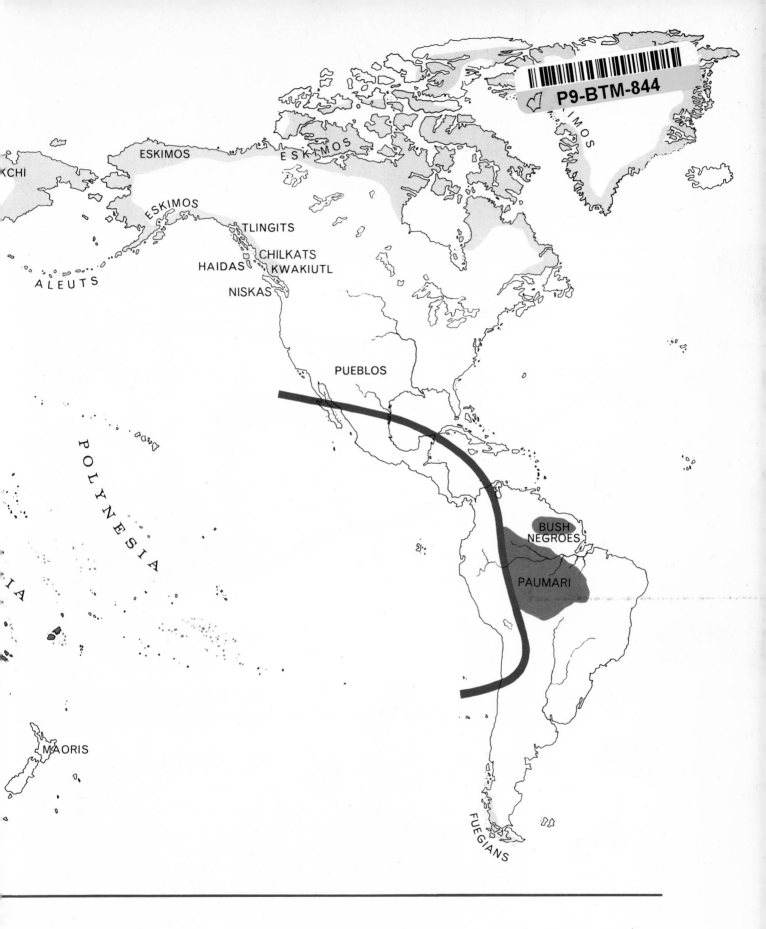

KCHI

ESKIMOS   E S K I M O S

ESKIMOS

ESKIMOS

TLINGITS

CHILKATS

HAIDAS   KWAKIUTL

A L E U T S

NISKAS

PUEBLOS

P O L Y N E S I A

I A

BUSH NEGROES

PAUMARI

MAORIS

FUEGIANS

Areas in which herdsman cultures still survive   Areas in which early farming cultures still survive

Prehistoric and Primitive Man

PREHISTORIC AND PRIMITIVE MAN

ANDREAS LOMMEL

Director of the Museum of Ethnology, Munich

145

PAUL HAMLYN · LONDON

General Editors

TREWIN COPPLESTONE   BERNARD S. MYERS
London   *New York*

PREHISTORIC AND PRIMITIVE MAN
Dr Andreas Lommel, Director of the Museum of Ethnology, Munich

THE ANCIENT WORLD
Professor Giovanni Garbini, Institute of Near Eastern Studies, University of Rome

THE CLASSICAL WORLD
Dr Donald Strong, Assistant Keeper, Department of Greek and Roman Antiquities, British Museum, London

THE EARLY CHRISTIAN AND BYZANTINE WORLD
Professor Jean Lassus, Institute of Art and Archaeology, University of Paris

THE WORLD OF ISLAM
Dr Ernst J. Grube, Associate Curator in Charge, Islamic Department, Metropolitan Museum of Art, New York

THE ORIENTAL WORLD
Jeannine Auboyer, Keeper at the Musée Guimet, Paris
Dr Roger Goepper, Director of the Museum of Far Eastern Art, Cologne

THE MEDIEVAL WORLD
Peter Kidson, Conway Librarian, Courtauld Institute of Art, London

MAN AND THE RENAISSANCE
Andrew Martindale, Senior Lecturer in the School of Fine Arts, University of East Anglia

THE AGE OF BAROQUE
Michael Kitson, Lecturer in the History of Art, Courtauld Institute of Art, London

THE MODERN WORLD
Norbert Lynton, Head of the School of Art History and General Studies, Chelsea School of Art, London

PUBLISHED BY
PAUL HAMLYN LIMITED · DRURY HOUSE ·
RUSSELL STREET · LONDON · W.C.2

© PAUL HAMLYN LIMITED 1966

PRINTED IN THE NETHERLANDS BY JOH. ENSCHEDÉ EN ZONEN
GRAFISCHE INRICHTING N.V. · HAARLEM

Previous pages: detail of figure 97, page 165

List of Contents

Colour Plates

Prehistoric 'Great Mother' figurine from Senorbi, Sardinia.
Limestone. Cagliari Museum.

Foreword

The numbers in the margins refer to the illustrations: heavy type for colour plates, italics for black and white illustrations. The letters refer to Charts A–J.

OURSELVES AND PRIMITIVE ART

It is impossible to draw a hard and fast line between the vanished primitive cultures of the past and those which still survive in all continents of the world except Europe, for those of the present are the heirs of the former. We have to remember that countless earlier primitive cultures have existed in Europe itself as well as in other continents, since the last Ice Age, and if we wish to gain an understanding of so-called primitive cultures and their art, we must consider the whole range of cultures, from the most primeval ones of which we have any knowledge, to those which we can see still existing in the world today. In this book, therefore, all such cultures, whatever the date of the period in history to which they belong, are treated as the single and, in a certain sense, timeless subject that the modern anthropologist can see them to be.

The history of art enables us, in fact, to identify and track down elements of cultural continuity in the form of the artistic motifs which one culture transmits to another, and of establishing the links that connect primitive peoples of any period both with their contemporary neighbours as well as with their predecessors. These interconnections, both in time and space, can be enthralling to study and they are given special attention in the plan of this book. In the chapters that follow, therefore, the reader will find many references to the diffusion of motifs across the globe, and often with what may seem to be rather unexpected links, not only between places which are separated from each other by, perhaps, vast stretches of ocean (for example, between Santo Domingo in the Caribbean and the Marquesas Islands in the Pacific, or between Indonesia and Madagascar), but also between peoples or cultures which are separated in time by the lapse of many centuries or even of millennia.

A few words of explanation are in place here to define the nature of the 'diffusionist' approach to art and civilisation. It can be summed up in the phrase, attributed to Leo Frobenius, 'the map cannot lie!' In other words, one takes some typical features of a given culture and marks on a map all the places where they occur. These features can be technical, such as weaving or the use of the wheel, or customs such as head-hunting, or artistic motifs such as the spiral. The result will be a map which shows the exact area of diffusion in each case. The culture in question can then be seen to be spread over the region where the various areas coincide on the map. In a similar way, relationships between cultures and the influences that have passed from one to another can be read from maps on which the relevant clues have been plotted.

The opening chapter provides a comparative survey of the nature of primitive cultures and of the 'high' or 'mature' cultures and defines the meaning of these terms. The earliest cultures of the human race are described on pages 14–46—those of the hunter peoples whose art appeared in Europe at the end of the last Ice Age, about thirty thousand years BC, reached its astonishingly accomplished peak in the famous cave paintings of south-western France and northern Spain about 12,000 BC, and spread throughout Africa, northern Asia, North and South America and Australia.

Animal representation (the 'zoomorphic' style) in rock paintings and engravings was the significant feature of the hunter peoples' art. Occasional human figures are found, but they were never rendered with the same naturalism as the lovingly observed animals were—man's interests were still focussed on the animal world on which his existence almost entirely depended, and his sense of superiority was not yet developed. The art of the early hunters died out in Europe many thousands of years ago, but it survived into our own time among the Bushmen in South Africa and Australian aborigines and was still produced in scattered regions of America until about the seventeenth century.

The next chapters deal with the next great human culture that succeeds the hunters, that of the food-producing farmers of the Neolithic and early Bronze Ages. Carved figures were their typical art-form, statuettes of humans replacing animals as the centre of interest. Agriculture originated in the Middle East in the eighth millennium BC, eventually providing the basis for the first mature cultures that emerged in the fertile crescent—Palestine, Syria and Mesopotamia. The traces of the spread of agricultural communities in Europe are found from the third millennium BC onward. The early agricultural culture of Europe received its main stimulus from the Middle East along the natural routes through the Mediterranean and up the Danube. The highest development of agriculturalist art, apart from the Middle East and, of course, in the high civilisations of India and China, was reached in South-East Asia during the first millennium BC.

Boundaries were naturally fluid and uncertain, and in many areas the two cultures, hunter and farmer, coexisted with mutual interaction between them. For example, the art of the hunter peoples was still flourishing in parts of the Mediterranean as late as the Neolithic period as can be seen in the coastal region of eastern Spain known as the

Levante. The rock paintings there combine the innovation of lively representations of the human figure—comparable with those found at the other end of the Mediterranean area, in the fortified Anatolian settlement of Çatal Hüyük, from about 6000 BC—with remnants of the hunters' animal style. This produced the style known equally as the 'Spanish Levant' or 'Second Hunter' style, which flourished between about 6000 and 2000 BC. Itself the distant product of influences from the mature cultures of the eastern Mediterranean, the Spanish Levant style was in turn transmitted to North Africa and was carried across the fertile regions of what is now the Sahara down as far as southern Africa.

The 'nomadic' style, which is the subject of pages 70–75, originated in the plains of northern and Central Asia as a continuation of the North-European hunter style, and was constantly involved in an exchange of influences with the mature cultures further south, in Iran and the Middle East. In the first millennium BC, the motifs of this style were brought to China by the invading nomads and were transmitted, as part of expanding Chinese influence, southwards to Indonesia. Because of its role in the diffusion of styles, the art of China will necessarily be discussed a good deal on pages 73–101, despite the fact that China has a highly-developed mature culture of its own.

Indonesia and the islands of the Pacific Ocean (Oceania) provide a sort of living laboratory for the study of the developed artistic styles of the food-producers and of their predecessors, the early hunters, and for this reason a whole chapter (pages 76–101) is devoted to this rich field. The squatting ancestor-figure in all its variations is the dominant motif of the agriculturalist style and because of its importance in tracing the currents and counterflow of cultural influences, this typical and sombrely expressive motif is fully discussed and illustrated on pages 102–134.

Ultimately, the motifs of the food-producers were diffused in altered forms across the Pacific Ocean to America and across the Indian Ocean to Africa.

In North and South America the remains of unadulterated hunter culture are slight, except among the Eskimos of the far north and some tribes in Tierra del Fuego at the southern tip of the continent. All American Indian peoples were influenced by the higher native cultures that surrounded them. The extant primitive cultures are mainly of agriculturalist origin and they, too, are overshadowed by the mature pre-Columbian cultures of Central America and the Andes. The waves of Oceanic, and even of direct Asiatic, influence which washed along the western coasts of the American continent have left their clear traces in the distribution of certain basic motifs. On pages 136 and 139 these will be looked at for clues to the stimuli which led to the great achievements of the ancient Mexicans and Peruvians. Africa offers a contrast to Indonesia, for in the latter region it is possible to find examples of both hunter and planter cultures in many different stages of development and interaction, while in Africa the two persist side by side, each keeping more or less separate in a clearly defined region of its own. An art of early hunter type runs down the eastern half of Africa to the very southern tip, while Negro art proper, which is of clearly agriculturalist origin, occupies the centre and west. Influences from the Middle East and from Mediterranean Europe have been transmitted to Negro Africa from very early times, though it is only in recent years that archaeological discoveries—which are described on page 162—have made it possible for us to understand how they came and what their effect was. A discussion of the impact of Negro art on the sensibility of modern western artists, and of the position of Negro art itself in the contemporary situation forms the concluding section of this chapter.

Introduction

THE MEANING OF 'PRIMITIVE' CULTURE

The historical study of man's development and achievements used to consider only the so-called 'high' or 'mature' cultures worthy of attention. 'Primitive' cultures were given summary treatment, if not ignored altogether. A change in attitude began with the scientific approach to the study of man and his origins in the middle of the nineteenth century. The value and relevance of man's prehistoric past was discovered, while the new museums and collections were filling with works of art, not only by early man, but by existing primitive peoples all over the world. It came to be recognised that in artistic achievement these societies may very well be the equal of mature ones, and indeed often surpass them.

The word 'primitive' is confusing, or at least ambiguous. By primitive cultures we understand on the one hand the prehistoric hunter and farmer societies from which the mature cultures of the ancient world developed, while on the other hand the same term is applied to existing cultures that survive alongside the mature cultures, though at a lower level of development. There is a real distinction that we must make between them. The former, the primitive cultures of prehistory, were vital and dynamic, engaged in a process of growth. The latter, however, lack any vitality, having remained static and, indeed, become almost ossified. It is only with great difficulty that they can contribute to, or become assimilated with, our modern world-wide civilisation.

The mature cultures of the ancient world emerged around 5000 BC in the Middle East, while those in India and China followed about a thousand years later. The rise of the mature cultures in the Americas began as late as 500 BC. Once the mature cultures were in existence the life of the primitive cultures began to undergo changes. The influence of the mature cultures on them was henceforward inescapable, but in the incomparably longer period of human development up to the fifth millennium BC, they occupied the whole world unchallenged and were able to exploit their inner resources of growth undisturbed and uninfluenced.

Though primitive cultures may be inferior to the mature cultures in their level of material culture and of economic and technical development, this is not true of their art. This puzzling and seemingly inexplicable fact only came to be clearly recognised in the late nineteenth century, when Europeans became aware of the attraction of exotic art, especially of Oceanic and Negro art. The first European cave paintings, which were discovered at Altamira in 1879 and in the Dordogne in the 1890s, proved that early man had been a consummate artist.

A history of world civilisation must take the interaction between primitive and more mature cultures into account. The latter develop in soil fertilised by one or more primitive cultures, bringing out and formulating in their art the concepts held by their antecedents. These versions are subsequently transmitted back to the primitive cultures in the course of trade, conquest or the general exchange of influence, and are then preserved in that form by the older cultures, often for considerable periods of time. This interplay governs the pattern of growth in primitive cultures, which are no longer left in a state of infancy or at one particular level of development. The influence exerted on them by the mature cultures is sometimes so strong that they are, so to speak, culturally stunted and often become incapable of further development. They are not strong enough to assimilate and go on to achieve more than they did before. In these cases, all the community's creative energies have been lost in the process of assimilation. This applies, for instance, to primitive cultures lying around the cradle of Chinese civilisation north of the Yellow River— with the interesting exception of Korea and Japan, where a native vigour enabled the people to absorb and digest the overwhelming influence of Han and T'ang dynasty China at the height of its expansionist self-confidence. In Korea and Japan new and individual cultures were fashioned which were able to develop in parallel with that of their gigantic neighbour, but other peoples, scattered through Manchuria, southern China, Annam and Taiwan (Formosa) remained fossilised. In many cases they adopted the outward forms of Chinese life, but otherwise merely stagnated.

The mature cultures run like a belt round the earth and divide the primitive cultures into two groups, one to the north and the other to the south. The former stretch from the Mediterranean and the Middle East by way of India, Indochina and Japan to Central America. They are all distinguished as such by the existence of towns, calendars, numbers and writing, and their economy is based upon agriculture. To the north and south there are belts of more primitive farming peoples, interspersed with groups of nomads whose way of life is an offshoot of the agriculturalist one blended with the traditions of the hunters. In the extreme north and south, in Siberia and the Arctic regions of Asia and America, in Australia and South Africa, small groups of hunters have survived until the present day in fairly isolated areas, where most of them are gradually being squeezed out of existence.

The ancestors of all human beings were at one time hunters, and the hunter cultures are extremely old. From a primeval stage of simple food-gathering, man seems to have developed into a hunter, a process which we think began about 50,000 BC, during the last Ice Age. Agriculture first appeared in the Middle East, though exactly where has not yet been determined. Excavations in Jericho and elsewhere make it likely, however, that the evolution from hunting to farming began about 8000 BC. The agricultural communities also spread out over the whole world, slowly absorbing the hunter cultures that stood in their way. Only one continent, Australia, was untouched by the early planter cultures and remained the preserve of hunters alone. The settlement of the Pacific Islands was carried out by planters who must have had seaworthy

3
1, 2, 4, 5,
6, 8, 13

End-
papers

boats by the first millennium BC. No such advanced means of navigation could have been available for the settlement of Australia by the hunters, which may have begun as early as 15,000 BC, and they appear to have used light bark canoes for the crossing.

AN OUTLINE HISTORY OF THE PRIMITIVE CULTURES

A history of human civilisation and its expression in art properly takes the early hunter cultures as its starting point, the art of which reached its climax in the cave paintings of south-western France and northern Spain about 12,000 BC. Even in the earliest stages of his cultural development as a nomadic hunter, man made enormous strides forward on the mental plane and we owe much of the present basis of civilised life to his achievements. It was as a hunter that man devised the earliest forms of religion, while the invention of language and the use of implements go back much earlier, to about half a million years ago when our ancestors were not even hunters but only food-gatherers. It is still hard for most people to imagine what the conditions of life of these early men were like or to realise the intellectual efforts made by these remote and ingenious individuals who were founding the human race.

There certainly were much older hunter cultures in Asia and Africa than in Europe. Deposits in the Olduvai
B Gorge in Tanzania have revealed hominids who were using stone chopping tools there probably a million years ago, while the human fossils found near Peking are 400,000 years old. For still unexplained reasons it is in Europe, however, that the artistic expression of the hunter peoples first makes its appearance. The outset of mankind's
2 artistic progress is attested by the famous ribbon-like lines drawn by human fingers across the wet clay wall of a cave at Altamira, which are dated about 30,000 BC. In order to understand what their art meant to them, one needs to get inside the mind of these early men and fortunately for us, the rock art of the hunter peoples spread slowly round the world to both Australia and southern Africa where rock art was actually being produced until very recently. The mentality of the early hunter peoples has been preserved by the Australian Aborigines and the South African Bushmen and also, to some extent, by the Eskimos. It is therefore possible for modern man to reconstruct sympathetically the concepts of the cave artists of Lascaux and Altamira.

Comparison of style and subjects make it possible for us to fix the chronology of the various stages of the diffusion of rock art. Between 9000 and 8000 BC, after the end of the last Ice Age in Europe, the change in climate radically altered mankind's living conditions. The increased warmth made the bare, frozen plains, on which the herds of game had existed, disappear, and forests began to cover them. The hunters, driven more or less back to food-gathering, were ready for the introduction of food production from the Middle East where the presence of suitable plants in a wild form made the region favourable for the

great discovery of domestication. The shift to food-production and farming in Europe was completed by about 2000 BC, by which time the influence of the mature Middle Eastern cultures was being felt in most parts—even, in the eastward direction, as far away as China. From now onward it becomes necessary to consider primitive cultures anywhere in the world in the light of their relationship to the mature cultures.

About 6000 BC, a new style of rock art came into being *16,17* in the western Mediterranean as a result of the nomadic hunters' contacts with the mature Middle Eastern cultures. To the old repertory of animal pictures were added human figures deriving from the contemporary cultures of Anatolia **18,19** (Çatal Hüyük), though they undoubtedly owe their particular elegance—especially when the human figures are in movement—to the hunters themselves. This 'Second Hunter style' spread across Africa and traces of it reached Australia by way of South-East Asia.

The only part of Europe where primitive cultures could persist after the rise and expansion of the Mediterranean civilisations was the far north, in the Arctic regions which are populated today by the nomadic reindeer-herding Lapps. Across the northern half of Asia the hunter way of life continued, though from about 2000 BC, mounted nomads, made mobile by their taming of the wild horse in the great central steppes, were able to develop the hunter culture to an even more advanced stage. They came into frequent contact with the mature cultures of the Middle East, of Europe and of China. Through China—whose E part in the diffusion of influences on primitive cultures is of great importance—the artistic motifs which the nomads had created were passed down to Indonesia.

Hunter cultures reached the American continent across the Bering Strait, perhaps as early as 20,000 BC. How the stimulus which later led to the discovery of agriculture and the creation of mature cultures in Mexico and the Andes was transmitted cannot be precisely determined, but it was probably brought over from Asia.

Africa remained largely outside the orbit of the mature cultures. North and East Africa were mainly occupied by J hunter peoples and nomads on whom Egypt had little influence. It seems likely that sometime in the first millennium BC, farmers from Indonesia reached East Africa by sea. In the second half of the first millennium BC a certain receptivity to the mature cultures of the Mediterranean is noticeable in West Africa.

MATURE CULTURES AND PRIMITIVE CULTURES

Thus the world over, from the beginning of history, we find mature cultures surrounded by groups of primitive ones which are more or less dependent on them, or have at any rate not remained at their original stage. What that was like we can only guess. Conversely, the great achievements of the mature cultures on the practical and intellectual levels are rooted in the primitive ones which they superseded, and among which the possibilities of progress were

CHART A

WESTERN EUROPEAN CLIMATIC AND CULTURAL TIME-SCALE

TEMPERATURE CURVE (Tentative Reconstruction) ← WARM COLD →	YEARS B.C.	GLACIAL OR INTERGLACIAL PERIOD	MAIN DIVISIONS OF PREHISTORIC EPOCH	ART	MAIN CULTURAL GROUPS AND TRADITIONS
	250,000		LOWER PALAEOLITHIC (EARLY OLD STONE AGE)	(FLINT TOOLS)	
		HOLSTEIN Interglacial period			CLACTONIAN (Swanscombe man)
	200,000				ACHEULIAN
					LEVALLOISIAN FLAKING
		RISS Glaciation			
	150,000				LEVALLOISIAN IN NORTH FRANCE AND BRITAIN
	100,000	EEMIAN Last Interglacial period			
					FINAL ACHEULIAN
		WÜRM Last Glaciation	UPPER PALAEOLITHIC (LATE OLD STONE AGE)	(BONE TOOLS)	MOUSTERIAN (Neanderthal man)
	50,000			FIRST ART OBJECTS	GRAVETTIAN AURIGNACIAN (modern Homo Sapiens)
	40,000				SOLUTREAN
	30,000			25000 BC	
	20,000				MAGDALENIAN
	10,000			ICE AGE ART 6000 BC	
	0		MESOLITHIC, NEOLITHIC	SECOND HUNTER STYLE	

first dimly conceived and anticipated. A primitive culture often incubates the basic ideas which the mature culture then brings to fruition. Art illustrates this process. There are certain ornamental motifs or styles which spread throughout the world during the primitive stages of human culture, which in many cases have been given a new lease of life in the art of the mature cultures. Numerous examples

D, G, H, I of the transmission of very primitive motifs will be shown in this book.

The early hunters' most typical form of expression is the animal style in rock paintings, and the zest with which they would depict the wild game on which they depended for life on the walls of their caves and rock shelters is quite characteristic of them, whether in Europe, Asia, Australia,

8 Africa or even South America. A feature which was not

11,12,60, quite so widely disseminated is the so-called X-ray style, in

5,6,7 which the animal's inner organs were also shown in the

10,11 picture.

The essential achievement of the mature cultures is the creation and imposition of order and form. People, state and city are subjected to an all-embracing concept of the universe. This made sense of the bewildering phenomena of the cosmos, of the earth, heaven and stars. The world in its order revolved round the sacrosanct figure of the ruler, there was an advanced form of religious belief and cult, and

a calendar based on astronomical observation and functioning with tolerable accuracy. These features are seen in the ancient Middle East and also in pre-Columbian America. Even primitive cultures are, of course, contrived constructions of the human mind too, but instead of imposing their order on nature around them, they try to assimilate man with his environment.

PRIMITIVE MAN

Primitive man lives in a more or less unconscious state. This does not mean that he is without understanding, but that he perceives his environment in a naive manner, and is therefore in a better position to experience it directly and, if he represents it artistically, to do so with freshness and vigour. Should he come into contact with a mature culture, he finds himself at the mercy of the religious, social and artistic formulas of the stronger cultures. In all primitive cultures great efforts are needed to assimilate these new and overpowering forms of organisation, philosophy, and artistic vision, to make sense of them and to turn them into something that the primitive culture can call its own.

The relationship between mature and primitive cultures has remained the same until modern times, but the gulf between them has widened. Modern 'high' cultures, that is to say, the technically developed industrial civilisations of

Europe and America, are no longer mature cultures in the old sense but something entirely new and different. Since the French Revolution these cultures have lost or surpassed the form and order of earlier high cultures, and they are now advancing, with an impetus hitherto unknown, towards a new system the character of which is as yet hidden from us. In the modern high cultures, order and form are conceived in economic and political rather than in religious or cultural terms. It is the difference in economic system that principally distinguishes the wealthy industrialised societies from those that we call 'under-developed'. The centre of gravity of the mature cultures has shifted to Europe and America. The northward regions of Canada and Siberia have been progressively swallowed up by them, while most of the 'under-developed countries' occupy the southern hemisphere, resulting in the curious division of the world into 'a rich north and a poor south', to use the late Pandit Nehru's expression.

The problem facing primitive cultures today is that of 'development'. For a long time—ever since mature cultures existed—primitive peoples have become passive recipients of mental stimuli from without, and until recent times no one had any thought of attempting a cultural exchange in the other direction. Now they are expected to model themselves economically and politically on the advanced cultures, but at the same time to strive to maintain an independent pattern of their own. This independence is usually conceived in economic or political terms, but is in reality cultural. The transformation of the 'under-developed' countries into modern industrialised nations *first* involves a cultural adjustment. Gradual cultural assimilation will bring economic and political assimilation in its train.

Modern industry needs an entirely different philosophical outlook from that appropriate to earlier and more primitive economic systems. It demands and educates a mind aware of modern scientific knowledge, and used to scientific method. The problem for the early hunter was to find and kill sufficient wild animals to assure his survival. Magic was the best he could do to try to influence the outcome of his chase. The problem for the primitive agriculturalist was to obtain a reliable supply of food by cultivating the soil and to secure the increase of the group to which he belonged. Increased fertility in plants as in man was his obsession and the object of his magic rites was to try to improve on it. In modern times the limits that there once were to such fertility seem to have vanished.

In earlier times it was always difficult to maintain a balance between the size of the population and the amount of food produced, but in the near future the ratio seems likely to become completely disproportionate. The rate of human population increase is greater than ever before and a situation could arise in which the area of land at our disposal and the fertility of our crops will no longer suffice to support human life. Neither in this respect nor in any other has the industrialised world found a stable order.

In the modern era we see the problem of order as one of achieving the just distribution of agricultural and industrial production among the various communities, peoples or classes. Man is only slowly coming to realise that an unchecked increase in population may one day lead to a production shortage. The obsession with reason, social justice and production will no doubt lead man to evolve a new order and way of life, but it will be a harsh order and a frugal life.

Yet even in this new order elements of the past will survive and continue to operate in the same way as they have always done. Such is the lesson of history. To understand what is happening in the world one must go back to first beginnings. To understand the history of civilisation it is necessary to penetrate the history of the mature cultures and analyse their progress, and to learn to recognise, without the benefit of written history, the course of change in the timeless existence of primitive cultures.

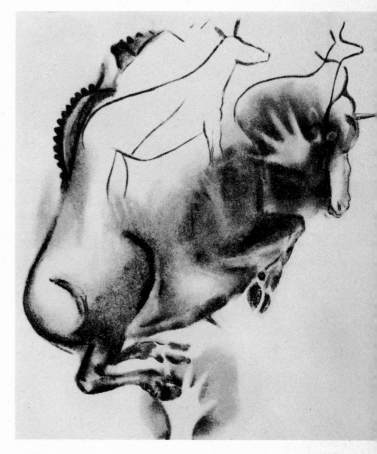

1. **Outlines of human hands superimposed on a bison and other animals.** Abbé Breuil's copy of an Aurignacian rock painting in red, *c.* 25,000 BC. Cueva del Castillo, Puente Viesgo (Santander). The French priest, Henri Breuil (1877–1961), was one of the world's greatest pioneers in the study and popularisation of the art of our Ice Age ancestors. His copies testify to his sympathy with their prehistoric masterpieces.

The Hunters

Dr L. S. B. Leakey, the British anthropologist, has already pushed the dawn of the human race back 1,800,000 years. Working in the Olduvai Gorge in northern Tanzania, he has excavated the fossil remains of a tool-using individual whom he calls *homo habilis*, who must have been more intelligent and mobile than the already known *homo zinjanthropus*, who lived in Africa some 1,750,000 years ago and eventually became extinct. *Homo habilis* lived alongside him down to about 800,000 BC, and is now regarded as the true ancestor of modern man, nature having abandoned other attempts to evolve a human species from the anthropoid family tree. Fossils of hominids (the ancestors of man, but not of the living apes) are found in early Pleistocene deposits at Olduvai, at Soan in India, at Chou-k'ou-tien near Peking, and in Java. At Olduvai there is also an early sequence of strata that illustrates the development of tool-making. It shows that man began to work with so-called pebble tools: a flake was simply struck off a pebble in such a way as to leave a sharp edge which was then worked to form a rough kind of cutting edge. At a very early stage Oldowan man already began to produce hand axes—pebble-tools which were shaped all the way round, and which are classified according to the typological sequence previously established by the finds in France.

The Pleistocene Age (from about two million years BC until about 30,000 BC) during which man as we know him was finally evolving, saw great fluctuations of climate on the globe, including several great ice ages, probably five in all, during which northern Europe was covered with glaciers and the tropical parts of Africa and Asia were more temperate than they are today. This made them favourable for the men of the early Old Stone Age (Lower Palaeolithic) to hunt in. In Africa their game consisted of hippopotamus, wild boar, wild sheep (Olorgesailie, near Nairobi, Kenya). In Spain (Torralba) it consisted of elephant, rhinoceros and aurochs (an extinct species of wild ox).

Towards the end of the Middle Pleistocene, about 250,000 BC, a change in the technique of producing hand axes took place in northern Africa. Less importance came to be attached to the nucleus or core of a pebble, formed by removing small flakes, and more to the actual flakes so detached. In a different technique the core was slightly curved into the shape of a tortoise-shell, and from this core flakes were then obtained which were used as tools on their own. This technique is termed 'Levalloisian' flaking. It probably spread from northern Africa to western Europe by way of the Middle East and southern Russia. In western Europe, some thirty to forty thousand years ago, the 'Mousterian' culture developed, and its chief exponent was Neanderthal man, who became extinct by the end of the Mousterian period. His importance lies in the fact that he seems already to have possessed a distinct form of burial: namely, interment in a crouching position, obtained by binding up the body of the deceased. As may be deduced from parallels among surviving primitive peoples, and even among some mature cultures, this position is intended to portray an embryo and suggests familiarity with the idea of rebirth after death.

The following period in western Europe is the 'Aurignacian', and is dated about 34,000–30,000 BC. It seems to have developed in western Asia and to have spread from there to the north, to Mesopotamia and to Afghanistan, and also to Europe *via* the Balkans. Exponents of this culture already made bone arrow-heads, and incised simple geometrical patterns on objects of stone and bone.

Aurignacian is in a sense the basis of the Gravettian culture (30,000–25,000 BC). This covered southern Russia and central Europe and extended to Spain, France and Italy. The exponents of Gravettian culture seem to have lived in open-air dwellings of their own construction. This was definitely the case in southern Russia at least. Their habitations were probably a sort of tent or lean-to. These people were above all mammoth-hunters, and artists as well. From the tusks they carved female figurines—some in a more or less naturalistic style, others very abstract. (We can assume that they also carved in wood which has not been preserved.) The abstract figures occasionally have strictly geometrical lozenge shapes carved on them.

The characteristic type of the naturalistic female figurines in mammoth-ivory is the famous 'Willendorf Venus'. The neglect of features in the face, and the emphasis on the swollen thighs and breasts and the prominent genitals, indicate that fertility was the almost obsessive theme of these figurines, examples of which have been found throughout the area of the Gravettian culture between South Russia and France. These carvings appear primitive, but the abstract geometric designs are already so accomplished that they look as though they come from a long tradition of workmanship, and this suggests that the Gravettian people had undergone a long process of development. The superb achievements of the cave artists of the Dordogne and northern Spain, to which we now come, may have been stimulated by an encounter with the art of this probably contemporary culture (the so-called 'Venus of Laussel', reproduced in colour in plate 14, would indicate a familiarity with the Gravettian 'Venuses').

Some thirty to forty thousand years ago, people in the caves of the Dordogne and northern Spain began drawing irregular lines with the fingers of one hand on their damp clay walls. These random lines developed into the outlines of animals and so into wall-paintings and modelled relief. During the 'Solutrian' period (about 20,000–15,000 BC) and the 'Magdalenian' (about 15,000–10,000 BC), these led to freely-drawn graffiti (wall engravings) with light colouring added. Man's abilities were now extending at a more rapid rate. Solutrian weapons and tools consist of beautifully worked stone spearheads of laurel-leaf outline, arrow-heads, bone awls and needles with eyes. Magdalenian man developed the technique further, making tools of bone or horn, harpoon-points, spear-throwers and small flint implements.

CHART B: EARLY MAN AND THE ICE AGES

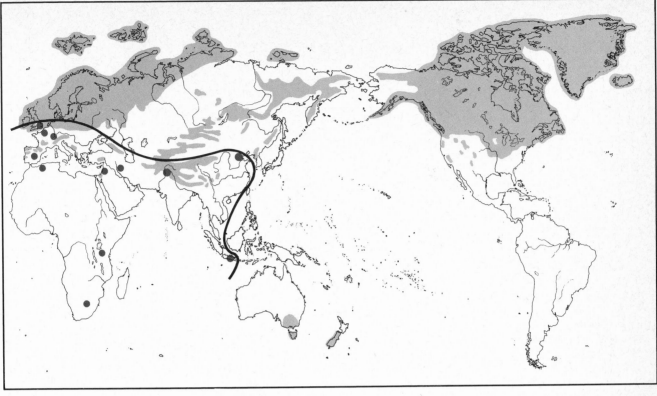

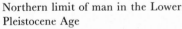
Northern limit of man in the Lower
Pleistocene Age

Ice-covered regions

●
Main sites of human fossil remains
(Clacton, Heidelberg, Torralba,
Olorgesailie, Olduvai, Sterkfontein,
Soan river, Chou-k'ou-tien, Java)

The style of the paintings is known, from the location of the caves, as 'Franco-Cantabrian', and it shows traces of several different influences, both from the earlier bone scratchings and carvings of the Aurignacian period, and from the figurines of the Gravettian culture. These paintings are the most exciting evidence of man's earliest achievement in art. The later ones, dating from about 12,000 BC, have attracted immense interest, but the explanation for their high quality mysteriously eludes us. Some people prefer to avoid any speculation altogether, for the problem poses unanswerable questions to the student of prehistory and, above all, to anyone with a naive belief in progress. For if early 'primitive' man was capable of producing such sophisticated works of art with his crude tools of stone and bone, he cannot by any means have been 'primitive' in an intellectual and artistic sense and must, on the contrary, have reached a peak of development that has not since been surpassed. This being so, artistic and mental development does not have to proceed parallel with advances in material civilisation. Acceptance of this hypothesis could revolutionise our accepted picture of human development as more or less straightforward progress.

Any attempt to penetrate the mental world of early man through his art confronts us with problems from the very outset. We should nevertheless try to discover what is was like, and can do so partly by studying specimens of his art and partly by studying the outlook of those hunter peoples

3,6,3

who have survived in remote parts of the world—in Australia, South Africa and South America. By exploring this world we may be able to establish what influence it had on later cultural developments.

THOUGHT AND ART OF THE HUNTER PEOPLES

The hunter peoples that are extant today are relics from prehistory, but over the millennia the influence of the mature cultures on them has certainly changed much of their social organisation and religious outlook. A modern man out hunting with his rifle and telescopic sights tells us little about the skills of ancient hunters, even though some of his procedures or customs may come down to him from the earliest times. In the course of time, hunting has become a matter of ever more complex equipment, and it is a far cry from modern firearms to the medieval cross-bow and net, and so to the prehistoric pit-fall. The earliest hunters had to compensate for their lack of equipment with a very high degree of skill, patience and sheer instinct —just as the modern hunter compensates for his lack of these qualities with the perfection of his equipment.

Hunting in the earliest times, when man was still weaker than the game he sought, must have required the maximum physical and mental concentration of which man was capable. This concentration, and man's relative position in the natural environment, produced a specific mental attitude. Man's inferiority had to be compensated for by an

2. **Musk-ox from the right-hand gallery at Altamira,**
Spain. *c.* 30,000 BC. l. (of drawing) 16 ft. 5 in. (5 m.). The
earliest works of art in the Ice Age were flowing lines drawn
with fingers in the damp clay. The contours may have
suggested a cheek and muzzle, and an identifiable outline
soon emerged from the 'doodles' (see drawing, below).

artificially induced sense of superiority, by an exaggeration
of the ego.

The hunter's attitude toward his environment is radically different from that of the primitive farmer. The farmer
sows and gathers in his crop; he is engaged in a productive
economy. He understands that you only get something if
you work for it. The hunter takes what he finds; he reaps,
as it were, without sowing. The primitive farmer, on the
other hand, has a more realistic frame of mind. He quickly
perceives that life grows out of death and that without
death there can be no life. The hunter does not produce—
he participates, he takes part in the life of his environment.
He kills the animals he needs but leaves their multiplication
to nature.

The hunter feels himself at one with nature. His vision of
world is as of a spiritual and material entity. Only very
gradually does he come to oppose himself to his environment, and so obtain an awareness of himself as an individual
being, distinct from the world of nature. He gradually
expresses this feeling of distinctness in his art, while re-
maining closely involved in nature. He attempts to impose
the power of his intellect upon his surroundings, for the
notion of a spiritual world which man can influence is
an invention of the hunter. But he still plays a natural part
in the natural order, whereas the farmer goes beyond this
equilibrium. From tillage he progresses to homestead and

village, from this to the city and so to the state. His system is an artificial one, opposed to nature. That of the hunter is natural and falls into place in the environment. Survivals of this early hunter outlook are found long afterwards in the mature cultures of Asia. In Chinese Taoism and in Japanese Shintoism, which are the indigenous religions of the country, nature and not man is the measure of all things. The corresponding art is not anthropomorphic but at first zoomorphic. In its later, advanced stages, the focus of such art turns to landscape. The human figure never plays an important part.

The hunter's entire mode of thought, as well as his art, is dominated by animals, which he sees as equal or even superior to himself. In this mythology the early hunter makes no distinction between man and beast: men may be transformed into animals and *vice versa*. In his art, human beings appear as animals, and later frequently as hybrid beings, such as occur later in Egyptian art and even in Classical times. Throughout North Africa there are rock pictures depicting human beings with animal heads. The Eskimos of Alaska are well known for their masks representing part-human, part-animal creatures, and American Indian masks from the North-West sometimes have an animal head outside which springs open to reveal another mask with a human face inside, symbolising the human soul inhabiting the animal.

The hunter's effort to subordinate himself to his natural environment is disturbed by the need to kill. This is the first serious step in the dissociation of man from his environment. The hunter kills animals in order to live, but this necessary slaying weighs more and more heavily upon his mind. It seems as though one of early man's major intellectual achievements is the attempt to become free from this burden. He finds a way of thinking death out of existence, and invents the concept of the immortal soul and of eternal life. The early hunter persuades himself that he is not really killing the animals themselves but only their bodies and that they can come to life again if their bones are looked after and treated with the correct magic.

This attitude leads man to reproduce animals through art. With the image he makes, he hopes to obtain control over the essential substance, the spiritual content, of the animal portrayed. The pictures themselves are intended to capture and contain the imagined powers of the animals concerned and are conceived of as a magical means of ensuring the supply of game. The complex ideas which early man elaborated can be studied, or at least guessed at, among the extant hunter peoples, even if perpetuated in a degenerate and abstract form. The concepts which these Stone Age people associate with the rock paintings are logically consistent, as is their entire cosmology, but for the modern European the underlying premises of their philosophy are difficult to grasp. Prehistoric man tried to comprehend his environment analogically, in parables, and to integrate himself into the life about him by the performance of symbolic actions.

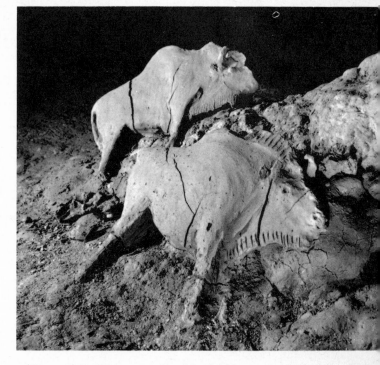

3. **Clay relief of bisons mating.** Magdalenian, *c.* 20,000–10,000 BC. h. (of male) 25 in. (63 cm.) h. (of female) 24 in. (61 cm.) Le Tuc d'Audoubert (Ariège), France. This famous naturalistic group by a Magdalenian artist was modelled in clay on a sloping slab of rock fallen from the ceiling. It clearly shows the magic purpose of the art of early man: the procreation of game.

It may come as a surprise that early men—the hunters of even the Early Stone Age (Lower Palaeolithic)—must have been thoughtful individuals, and not at all the 'primitive savages' that they were once thought to have been. They were backward only in the sense that they stood at the beginning of human development, not in the sense of being simple or half-animal, as they used to be portrayed in popular reconstructions on the basis of the first fossil skulls. It may not be easy for modern man to do justice to these prehistoric people and to understand their mental make-up, but the rock art which they have left us ought to help in finding a way to them.

No one disputes the fact that the rock paintings are great and unique works of art, yet some people still seem reluctant to admit that those who produced these works must also have been men of unique intellectual accomplishment, in a word, great artists who are comparable with the dominating figures of historical times.

THE IMPORTANCE OF SHAMANISM

A shaman (the word is of Tungusian origin) is not the same as the medicine-men, witch-doctors or magicians who may be found among all primitive groups up to the present time. He is, instead, a particular type of individual who survives among some hunters in northern Siberia and among the Eskimos, and has left traces in Australia and

18

CHART C: ROCK ART IN WESTERN EUROPE

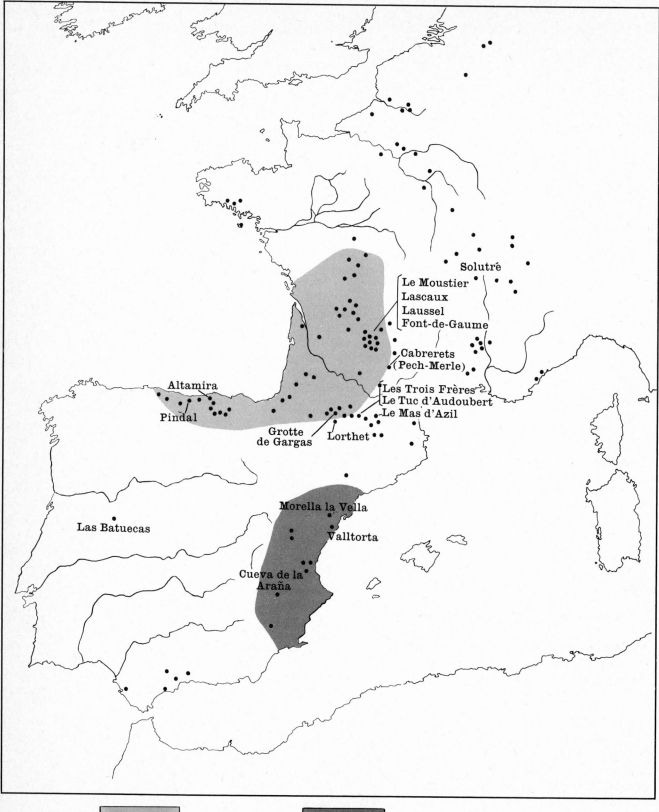

Le Moustier
Lascaux
Laussel
Font-de-Gaume

Solutré

Cabrerets
(Pech-Merle)

Altamira

Les Trois Frères
Le Tuc d'Audoubert
Le Mas d'Azil

Pindal

Grotte
de Gargas

Lorthet

Morella la Vella

Las Batuecas

Valltorta

Cueva de la
Araña

Prehistoric sites

Area of Franco-Cantabrian rock art

Area of the Second Hunter style
(Spanish Levant)

Africa. He is a man who combines functions and abilities which in the modern world have become divorced from each other, being simultaneously priest, doctor and artist. As may be proved from the art of surviving shamans, a large number of even the very early Franco-Cantabrian rock paintings is 'shamanistic'—that is to say, they were produced by shamans and derived from their modes of thought. To understand the rock paintings it is therefore necessary to explain more precisely what a shaman is.

Among many primitive peoples shaman and medicine-man perform identical functions and use identical psychological techniques, but each has a very different character and mentality. The medicine-man appears among all primitive groups, almost without exception. His function is first and foremost that of a physician, but in nearly every case he holds a key position within the group. Often he is at the opposite pole to the chief. Sometimes both functions are assumed by a single individual. In most cases the part he plays surpasses that of a physician and comes closer to that of a pastor or priest—or to that of the modern psychologist.

The shaman also carries out the functions of priest as well as physician, but unlike the medicine-man, he always acts in a self-induced state of trance. When he conjures up spirits or makes attempts at healing he never operates in a state of complete consciousness, but usually in a state of ecstasy. Accordingly, one finds psychic phenomena such as telepathy, clairvoyance, mysterious disappearance and re-appearance and the like. With the medicine-man these activities belong rather to the realm of hocus-pocus. They are performed in order to enhance the effect of suggestion induced among the audience. The shaman, on the other hand, experiences all these psychological phenomena on his own person with great intensity. With the medicine-man one can detect an unmistakable desire for power. The shaman, however, is a more complex personality. In many instances he becomes a shaman, not by his own volition, but because he is forced to by a feeling that it is his vocation. The shaman exerts a great influence upon those around him, and his social function is no doubt that of controlling and preserving their psychological equilibrium, but he exercises this function not because he seeks power but as a result of his own psychological development.

The psychological differences between them are seen in the course of events that leads them to adopt their respective functions, in the differences in their personalities and their attitude toward the world about them and in the different techniques which they use to influence their environment. Finally there is the fact that the shaman is often an active artist—a singer, dancer, decorator and stage-manager—activities which are alien to the medicine-man. The shaman often takes up his duties involuntarily. He seems to be under a pressure from which he can escape only by becoming a shaman. Siberian accounts make it clear that the prospective shaman has no conscious desire at all for this office but is forced into it 'by the spirits', and

finally enters upon it in order not to perish. The budding young shaman is a sick man. He suffers from psychopathic or epileptic disorders and is very often physically ill as well. Despite frequent attempts to do so he is unable to evade the demands made upon him by the spirits, who aggravate his condition more and more. He finds himself in a dilemma which he can solve only by dying or by assuming the office of shaman.

In modern terms, he is suffering from a psychosis which becomes steadily worse and compels him to adopt an attitude of mind and a mode of action laid down by tradition, or else to perish. The psychosis may be so severe that the one afflicted is destroyed by it if he is not cured in time. The healing process is itself regarded as a kind of death and rebirth. The potential shaman senses how the spirits kill, dismember and consume him. During his cure he feels the various parts of his body join together again and his personality become restored. The psychosis from which such people suffer must have a very long history. At a very early date men must already have discovered means of healing it and have given to these means certain traditional forms. In contrast to the medicine-man, who takes up his profession as a healthy individual, filled with a lust for power, the shaman at first appears as an invalid, who has to pass through a definite process of psychological development before he is cured. The social functions of the shaman develop, so to speak, as an ancillary of this healing process. It is these social functions that of course make him so significant for the group to which he ministers. The healing process, which builds up to a prolonged but repeatedly interrupted trance, is incorporated in the local religious tradition. In his unconscious state the shaman sees mental images, and the traditional cosmology of his community, their mythology, assumes a new poetic and artistic form in his mind's eye. Particular art forms and styles can be attributed to the influence of shamanism, and methods and techniques, such as the drama, the dance, the recitation of odes and the use of masks, probably originated to a large extent in the self-healing process which the potential shaman had to undergo.

Members of the tribe regard their shaman as one who, while in a trance, can temporarily detach his 'soul' from his body by the force of his will and journey into the 'nether world' or the 'world beyond', where he creates (on a psychological plane) the prerequisites for events that take place in the real world. Shamanism as a technique and outlook must have developed at a time when man no longer felt himself to be one with nature in an organic entity, and had become aware of a separate physical and mental existence. Overpowering psychic experiences began to be seen, not as a personal accident, but as the projections of alien spirits, invisible to the ordinary eye, which had supposedly taken possession of his body. In anthropological terminology, shamans are classed as 'frenzied priests'. The phenomenon of frenzy only occurs at the stage of human development when man is not yet fully aware of the effect

4. **Engraved outline of a bear,** drawn over with chalk. Arctic art (northern group), *c.* 5000–2000 BC. l. (of bear) 7 ft. 4 in. (220 cm.). Finnhagen, Nordland, Norway. On a bare outcrop of rocks exposed by the retreat of the glaciers that had once ground them smooth, the early hunters of Scandinavia chiselled and polished—with stone tools—this fine naturalistic outline of the beast they respected most. It is rare to find an example of the monumental animal style so far north.

of his own mental processes. The concept of a soul which can be detached from a man's body, can continue to live after death, and can later be provided with a body again, is of fundamental significance in the emergence of shamanism. Both men and animals had souls which were subject to the same laws governing separation and reincarnation. The magic of the early hunter peoples, which is of very ancient origin, is entirely based on the idea that the souls of animals can be caught and killed. It followed that the animals could be killed by the same means.

In order to secure success in hunting expeditions the shaman betakes himself, or more accurately sends his soul, into another world, while 'his body lies as though dead' There he either hunts animal spirits or negotiates with the 'mistress of the animals', a spirit to whom all animals of the chase owe submission. Drawings, poems and dances all serve the shaman as means of describing this journey into the nether world. The secret of successful hunting magic consists in mimicry. The successful expedition is visualised mentally by the shaman in advance, and represented with such conviction that, when the hunters set out, they do not even conceive the possibility of the expedition failing. In stalking and taking prey they are endowed with the assurance of sleep-walkers. A shaman has the power to ward off illness and accident in so far as this is possible through influencing the patient's psychological attitude. The influence he exerts upon the well-being of his fellow-tribesmen consists in arousing among them feelings of self-reliance and self-confidence or the absolute belief in their impending success.

Much emphasis has rightly been placed on the social function of the shaman as magician, priest and physician. His artistic role and accomplishments, however, may be more important, at least from an individual if not a social point of view. They are, of course, vital for an understanding of the content of rock paintings. The entire process of becoming and operating as a shaman is essentially a creative artistic process. First, an invalid cures himself by bringing his latent artistic abilities into play. Thereafter his social effectiveness is in being able to repeat the process at will on specific occasions. He begins by putting himself into a trance, for which he uses various means, generally making monotonous repetitive sounds with a drum or rattle, accompanied by dance movements. He loses consciousness and gives expression to his creative subconscious mind.

The shaman can vividly 'realise' the community's cosmology to his audience. It also seems that in his trance the shaman is better able to transfer to the physically and mentally ill among his audience the healing power which he has acquired. The shaman experiences his state of trance, during which he fashions images in his mind, as a communication with spirits. He visualises the shifting of his level of consciousness as a 'journey into the beyond'. The 'spirits' and the 'journey into the beyond' are never visualised nor conceived as manifestations of his personal being. 'Communication with the spirits' seems to be an activation of regions of the consciousness which the shaman cannot bring into play while he is in a normal state. This is evidently a psychic technique, probably very ancient in origin, still to be rediscovered by modern psychologists, and which is apparently an age-old remedy for certain depressive states of mind.

Our knowledge of shamanism is usually based on accounts dealing with Siberia and North America, but once we define a shaman as one who can operate only when in a trance, the phenomenon of shamanism is seen to be far more widespread. It seems to occur in nearly every region where early hunter cultures have survived until recent times: among the Eskimos, the Lapps of northern Scandinavia, in North and South America, various parts of Africa, and on the north-western fringe of Australia. Among many surviving hunter peoples the soul—especially of animals—appears to be associated with certain parts of the body, such as the bones or hide, and by preserving such parts it is believed that one can bind to oneself the souls of the animals concerned, make them well disposed towards one, give them a new incarnation, and cause them to be hunted as live animals. Archaeological evidence of the early existence of this concept has been found in the west of Switzerland, where the skulls of cave bears, which must once have been mankind's most important prey, were ceremonially buried during the Alpine Palaeolithic phase. Vestiges of bear ceremonies are still found in Siberia and among the Ainu of northern Japan. Ice Age rock paintings, such as those at Lascaux, already included representations which we can interpret as shamanist.

THE ART OF THE FRANCO-CANTABRIAN CAVES

Western European art began, probably between 30,000 and 25,000 BC, as simple 'doodles' drawn with fingers on damp clay. Eventually, the early people of the caves seem to have come to pick out recognisable sketches of animals from the casual and meandering lines. The style of the first of the three phases into which fully developed cave art can be divided consisted of black outline drawings of animals with a thin monochrome filling. In the second phase, the outlines were filled in with two-colour modelling. In these earlier pictures, rocky projections, areas of natural shadow and suchlike features of the rock face were often made use of, and may even have provided a starting-point for the artist. The polychrome paintings of Altamira and Font de Gaume belong to the third and most impressive phase. The high degree of naturalism in the drawing and the impressionist effects of movement and volume were, amazingly enough, achieved with only the most basic materials—charcoal and earth colours. Modern man might well be humbled by looking at and trying to explain the precocious accomplishment of the earliest artists of the human race.

Geometric patterns and signs occupy only a small part of this art. They are relatively scarce and were probably added to the animal pictures for the magical purposes already described. Geometric designs were sometimes scratched on the Gravettian ivory figurines of the same period in eastern and Central Europe, and they also occur on the small painted pebbles, of uncertain use, which have been found in southern French caves and dated to the Azilian period (about 8000 BC).

Ice Age cave paintings were first rediscovered at Altamira in Spain in 1879 by the twelve-year-old daughter of Baron Sautuola. She had gone with her father into a cave he was exploring and noticed paintings on the ceiling which he had overlooked. The consequences of her discovery marked a new epoch in our understanding of European thought and art. It was not easy to arrive at the right interpretation of the pictures. The explanations given by Australian aborigines who still produce or renew rock pictures not only show how mistaken Europeans can be in their interpretations, but are themselves at times obscure to the modern western mind. For example, rock pictures in a straightforwardly naturalistic style may contain geometric designs which turn out to be stylised representations of certain objects made of sticks which the aborigines use in their rituals, and which are, in their turn, symbolic of animals or foodstuffs of importance to their existence. This unconcerned infusion into a naturalistic painting of abstract emblems from another art-form—the realm of religious cult and its close relative the drama—is also found in some of the early rock pictures of western Europe.

Shadowy recollections of the cave paintings seem to have persisted through the millennia among the population of Spain and south-western France, almost until modern times. When Dr. Herbert Kühn, the author of *The Rock Pictures of Europe*, visited the Valltorta gorge paintings in Spain in 1923, the villagers of Alboacer refused to accompany him for fear of the spirits they believed haunted the place. Dr. Kühn also pointed out that haunted rock pictures were mentioned in a comedy written by Lope de Vega in 1598. They were situated in the Las Batuecas country, between Salamanca and Cáceres, and were, in fact, found there in 1909. The first Borgia pope, Calixtus III (1455–1458), was a Spaniard who had long been archbishop of Valencia, and it is recorded that during his pontificate he forbade the celebration of religious rites in an unidentified Spanish cave that was decorated with pictures of horses.

The area inhabited by the Basque people *(Vascones)* as late as Roman times coincided broadly with the sites of the Franco-Cantabrian caves. Researches into Basque folklore by José-Miguel de Barandiaran have revealed faint traces of a knowledge of the prehistoric cave paintings. The myths which testify to them are concerned with ghosts, animal apparitions, red bulls, cows and occasionally also with horses, birds and snakes. The most significant myths, however, concern spirits which were said to appear to man in half-animal, half-human form—above all, a female spirit called Mari. She lived in the caves and rules the thunder, but was well-disposed toward mankind. Mari usually appeared in the form of a beautiful woman, except that she had talons in place of feet—a feature shared by male spirits called Maide, with whom female spirits called Lamin were associated. Mari's herds of deer had to be accounted for and if any human being dared to make a false return to her

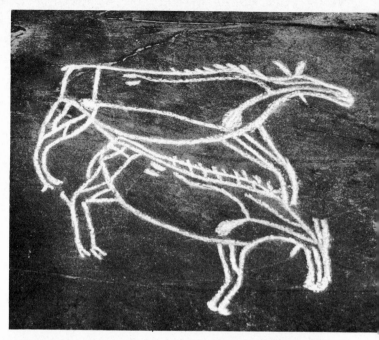

5 (above). **Copy of the incised profile of a trout.** Engraving on a bone found at Lorthet (Htes. Pyrénées), France. Late Magdalenian, *c*. 13,000–6000 BC. l. 3½ in. (8.5 cm.). (After Graziosi, *Palaeolithic Art*, pl. 50e.) The earliest examples of the X-ray style are found on fragments of bone in S.-W. France. The Ice Age artist marked the spots of a trout's skin but added the digestive tube as well.

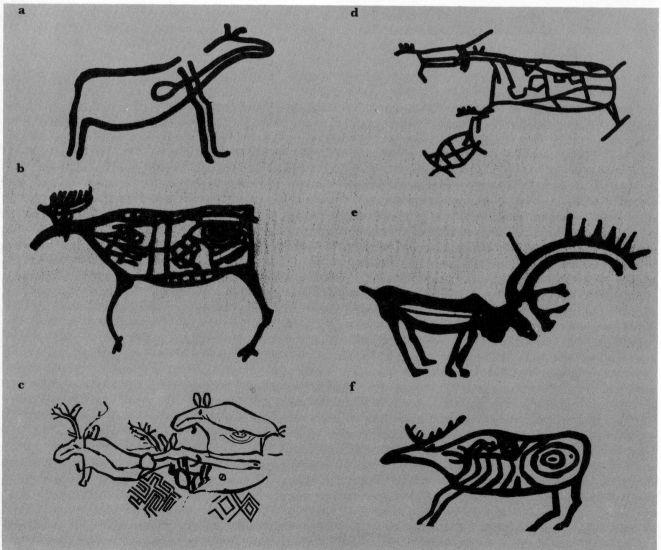

6. **Rock engraving of elks mating,** drawn over with chalk. Arctic art (eastern group), *c.* 5000–2000 BC. l. (of figures) 28 in. (70 cm.). Kløtefoss, Gjeithus, Modum, Buskerud, Norway. The vertebrae, aorta, heart and other organs are quite confidently drawn in this northern European example of the early hunters' X-ray style. The magic significance of the scene is the same as that of figure 3.

7. **Variation and spread of the X-ray style,** seen in copies of six primitive animal representations. Plate 12 shows a North American example. (*a*) Arctic art rock engraving at Evenhus, North Trøndelag, Norway (central group). l. of animal *c.* 2 ft. (64 cm.) (*b*) Arctic art rock engraving of an elk at Åskollen, Vestfold, Norway (eastern group). l. of elk, 5 ft. 4 in. (175 cm.) (*c*) Arctic art rock painting in red of reindeer with geometric designs at Hinna, Møre og Romsdal, Norway (central group). About 5000–2000 BC. l. of figures, 9 ft. 6 in. (280 cm.) (*d*) Arctic art rock engravings of a stag or reindeer and a fox at Skoger-veien, Drammen, Buskerud, Norway (eastern group). l. of figure, 4 ft. 4 in. (132 cm.) (*e*) Lapp painting of a reindeer on a Shaman's drumskin. (*f*) Rock engraving of a reindeer at Sakachi, Amur-Ussuri rivers region (Maritime Kray, USSR).

8. **Three deer painted in yellow and red, with the outline of a fish at Cêrca Grande,** Minas Gerais, Brazil. As the hunter way of life spread across the world, it was always accompanied by rock art in the naturalistic animal style—often works of great elegance, like these deer in a prehistoric rock shelter only 200 miles from Rio de Janeiro.

she would punish the deceit by causing the unnumbered deer to vanish. Mari and the Lamin probably preserved characteristics of the more ancient 'mistress of the beasts' and they also resembled in some ways the *akkas* or 'nether-world goddesses' of Lapp mythology (see page 44).

'The shamanism of the prehistoric hunters depended on the belief that images perceived inwardly by the power of imagination could influence the course of objective events.' An explicit revival of this mental technique was fostered by St Ignatius de Loyola (1491–1556)—a Basque from Gui-puzcoa. His *Spiritual Exercises* were constructed on a series of 'Meditations', or mind-pictures of scenes of Christ's redemption of mankind, which could be practised, under a 'spiritual director', by all the faithful. Miguel de Una-muno (1864–1936), the Spanish poet and philosopher, and a Basque as well, discerned a connection between the figure of Don Quixote, living in the world of his imagina-tion and ignoring reality, and St Ignatius. Here, in the Catholic saint, Unamuno may have brought into the open a concept which had survived subconsciously in Basque traditions, and which has contributed a basic trait to the Spanish national character. Its origin would thus go back to prehistoric times and to shamanistic beliefs.

Once we have established the fact that the outlook of shamanism helps us to elucidate the meaning of the Ice Age and subsequent rock pictures, there is no good reason

why we should not also be able to discover shamanistic features in the folklore of southern France and northern Spain, such as we are conditioned to expect only in the mythology of northern Europe.

DIFFUSION OF THE ANIMAL STYLE

Having originated in the caves of south-western France and northern Spain in the period between about 40,000 and 12,000 BC, rock painting in the hunters' style began to spread out over the whole world from about 15,000 BC on-ward, and it becomes possible to speak, from now on, of a universal animal style. The earliest representations are outlines incised in stone and burnished. Drawings of this nature are to be found over an area extending from the Franco-Cantabrian area, by way of North Africa, to southern Africa where traces of the oldest pictures were preserved alongside a tradition which continued down to the arrival of the Europeans. Some of the last examples ever made between 1820 and 1870 at Bellevue in the Drakens-berg depict British soldiers in uniform hunting eland.

Paintings in the hunter style also occur in Norway and Siberia. The quality of the hunter peoples' art often deteriorated as it spread, but the basic motifs and, to some extent, the monumental scale of the pictures, remained the same as they had been in the caves of western Europe. In Siberia and northern Africa, the early hunter style animal

9. **Leaping wild ox with 'trap' and two ponies.** Magdalenian, *c*. 15,000–10,000 BC. Copy of a rock painting on the right wall of the axial gallery at Lascaux (Dordogne). l. (of ox) 68 in. (170 cm.). The ox was painted in black monochrome over another figure in red. The ponies below were thickly outlined in black and then filled in with brown. The so-called 'trap' was added in red ochre. The hunting-magic ritual of pictorially 'capturing' an animal's soul in this manner is also illustrated in plates 5 and 6.

representations are always noticeably bigger than those of later periods.

The animals depicted are large species like bears or bison, replaced in Africa by *bubalus antiquus* (an early buffalo) and rhinoceros, and the hunting-magic element is usually strongly emphasised. There are pictures of animals with arrows flying into them, while some pictures are actually stabbed with sharp points. Abstract signs which may signify traps are drawn beside a number of animals (see page 44).

Rock art spread only slowly northward, and probably not by a direct route. It eventually reached Scandinavia between 6000 and 2000 BC, Siberia by 2000 BC and by the first millennium BC appeared in the Far East. Thence it passed on to America, perhaps as late as about 500 AD. During the course of these migrations the animal style frequently mingled with other styles. It stimulated the art of the early food-producing peoples of northern Anatolia, and even of the city-dwellers of Shang and Chou dynasty China, and in return received stimuli from them. It can be assumed that all animal motifs, wherever they turn up, are originally derived from the Stone Age hunter style. In some areas where there are now hardly any vestiges of the hunter style, the custom of painting on rocks has been preserved.

The aboriginal people of Australia, as a result of their isolated geographical position, are a special case. The hunter style probably arrived about 2000 BC, but contact with the early food-producers of Oceania led to the absorbtion from them of various stylistic features. The early hunter motifs became more abstract, as anyone familiar with recent aboriginal art will know, except in Arnhem Land in the north of the continent where the hunter traditions lasted longer and the older naturalistic character in rock paintings was more clearly retained.

In North America there is little hunter rock art to be seen apart from some fine examples in California. In Central America it has been obscured by the styles of rock painting produced by the later mature cultures of Mexico, while in the northern part of South America (Guyana and Ecuador) there are sprinklings of unmistakable motifs from the Pacific islands. A few examples of rock paintings in the pure hunter style are found in most parts of South America.

North Africa contains the numerous and well-preserved rock paintings and engravings of the Atlas mountains and, most famous of all, of the Tassili highlands in the central Sahara. These are the work of generations of hunters and

nomads who inhabited these once fertile regions with their abundant wild game. Later in the same region a mixture of hunter style with provincial Roman art occurs.

The hunter culture continued to be the way of life of the peoples of Siberia and northern Asia until well into historical times. Mounted nomads such as the Scythians, Sarmatians and Huns were the heirs of their art, which had radiated as far as Mesopotamia and had been reflected back in a modified form. New animals like the lion, unknown to the northern hunters, were represented, and positions and groupings were introduced which had never found a place in the ancient rock paintings. The animal style of the steppes as we know it is displayed in the magnificent bronze ornaments and objects from the Ordos region of north-western China and the Minusinsk basin of eastern Siberia, clearly deriving from the hunter style, but Middle Eastern innovations like animals in fighting groups reveal a change in outlook. The original purpose had been magical and the hunter style had been based on observation—now, decoration becomes its purpose. Variants of the animal style of the mounted nomads extend to India and China, and by way of China, continue in often undetected forms through Indonesia and Oceania.

STYLES OF THE HUNTER PEOPLES

Within the vast artistic output of the hunter peoples certain persistent motifs can be distinguished and their development traced. The three most important of these are

(Continued on page 41)

1 (opposite). **Animals of the chase.** *c*. 15,000–10,000 BC. Cave painting. h. (of deer) *c*. 31½ in. (80 cm.). Lascaux, France. Added to or renewed over long periods of time—perhaps when each hunting season came round—these masterly red ochre and charcoal drawings of animals were made as part of a magic ritual, which the hunters believed gave them control over the spirits of the animals on which their existence depended. The game would then come to them willingly. The deer in this section of Lascaux figures are probably later additions to the rock surface than the large-scale horse and cattle above—all of them having survived underground as some of the finest examples of the early art of the Ice Age. The enigmatic red marks at the left (and similar marks in plates 4, 5, 6 and 8) have been interpreted by some experts as abstract symbols for traps, applied near the pictures for magic purposes.

2 (opposite, above). **Horses.** *c*. 20,000 BC. Cave painting. l. (of horses) 11 ft. (3.4 m.) Pech-Merle, France. The large coloured spots inside and around the outline of the wild horses were probably put there in the belief that they increased the animals' fertility. Australian aboriginals still make rock pictures out of a conglomeration of dots, or chip them on stones below the rock pictures—they call this 'knocking the spirit-power out of the stone'. The meaning of the silhouette prints of human hands is not understood, but were almost certainly connected with hunting magic (see plates 84, 85).

3 (opposite, below). **Bison.** *c*. 12,000 BC. Cave painting. l. (of bison) 31½ in. (80 cm.). Altamira, Spain. In spite of their rather small scale, the procession of these massive creatures along the rock wall makes a most realistic impression. The Altamira caves contain the master-pieces of the Ice Age style, and the effect of ponderous strength which was achieved here through economical drawing and impressionist colouring anticipates the techniques of many 20th-century painters.

4 (below). **Man in a bird's-head mask attacked by a wounded bison.** *c*. 15,000–10,000 BC. Cave painting. h. 55 in. (140 cm.). Lascaux, France. This vivid and gory scene can be explained with the help of shamanist legends that survived in Siberia until modern times. Battle is joined between two rival shamans, one in the guise of a bison and the other with a bird's head. The wand with the figure of a bird on top suggests that the prostrate shaman's 'spirit-helper' appeared in bird form. A spear seems to have pierced the bison's flank and its bowels may be seen gushing from the wound.

5 (opposite, above). **Horses and ibexes.**
c. 15,000–10,000 BC. Cave painting. h.
c. 31½ in. (80 cm.). Lascaux, France.
The prominently drawn 'traps' here and
in plate 6 may not have been intended
literally but as magical objects with which
to trap the animals' souls (see plate 8).

6 (opposite, below). **Horse.** *c.* 15,000–
10,000 BC. Cave painting. l. (of horse)
55 in. (140 cm.). Lascaux, France. The
firm drawing and polychrome modelling
of this burly breed of early pony—a
favourite prey of man in the Magdalenian
period—effectively suggest the animal's
energy. The hunting-magic purpose of
the picture is obvious: apart from the
'trap' emblem, the artists added flying
arrows.

7 (below). **Eskimo inua mask,** S.-E.
Alaska. Probably 19th century. Painted
wood and feathers. h. 19 in. (48 cm.).
André Breton Collection, Paris. The soul
of a salmon is represented. By wearing
such masks in dances and ceremonies, the
hunters believed they could increase their
magical control over animals' souls and so
over their real bodies. The seven pendants
are stylised reductions from the fish-shape,
and reinforced the power of the mask
magic (see also plates 9, 10).

8. Painted and incised chequerboard pattern. *c.* 15,000–12,000 BC. Cave painting. 9½ × 8¾ in. (24 × 22 cm.). Lascaux, France. If, as seems likely, this design is an elaboration of the 'trap' motif, (see plates 5, 6), it would make it a very rare example in Ice Age art of an abstraction constituting the whole picture on its own. Elsewhere, the 'traps' always accompany animal representations. The colours and texture are close in feeling to the work of some 20th-century abstract artists—particularly of Paul Klee.

9 (opposite). **Kuskokwim Eskimo mask.** Late 19th century. Painted wood and feathers. h. 28½ in. (72 cm.). André Breton Collection, Paris. An extraordinarily powerful evocation of the movement of whales through the ocean is achieved by the sweeping plastic form and airy decoration of this mask. It represents a 'spirit-helper' conducting a school of great white whales to the hunters and was actually worn by a shaman in the ceremonies. The symbolic pendants, like those in plate 7, were to augment the mask's inherent power.

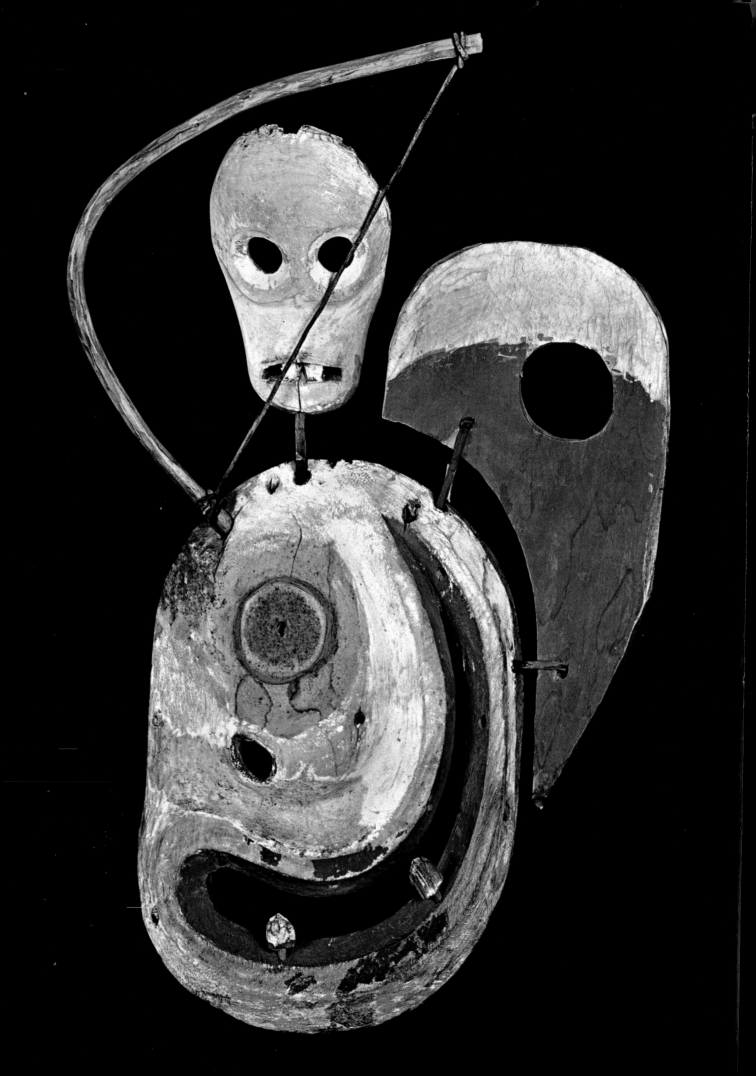

10 (opposite). **Eskimo mask, from S.-W. Alaska.** 19th century. Painted wood. h. *c.* 15 in. (38 cm.). Museum of Anthropology, University of California. The grotesque vision of a 'spirit-helper' seen by a shaman in a trance has been translated into concrete form with amazingly simple means. The economy and dynamic line of the mask give it an affinity with modern western art, but in fact it is free from any European influence. The twisted mouth motif is found else-where in North America, notably in the old Iroquois 'false-face' masks.

11 (left). **Fragment of an embroidered mantle border.** From the southern coastal area of Peru. Late Paracas (Necropolis) style (400 BC–400 AD). Wool. l. 21 in. (53 cm.). Robert Woods Bliss Collection, National Gallery of Art, Washington, D.C. Two unmistakable motifs in the larger human spirits on this pre-Columbian embroidery link it directly with sources in the South Pacific and, ultimately, in Neolithic China. The prominent rib-cases are a motif symbolising the spirit of a dead ancestor which comes from Yang Shao painted pottery (2200–1700 BC) *via* the Marquesas (200 BC) to South America. The bent knees indicating a figure in movement is a Polynesian variant of the early squatting ancestor figure that originated in southern China during the second millennium BC.

12 (below). **Pueblo Indian clay vessel** (Zuñi tribe). 19th century. h. 9 in. (23 cm.). Museum für Völkerkunde, Munich. The ancient Americans never knew the potter's or any other wheel, and this well-proportioned bowl was formed entirely by hand. The painted decoration successfully combines two distinct styles —a fluent abstract design based on western Asian spiral motifs, and a pure hunter motif of naively depicted natural-istic deer in the clearest possible X-ray style. The lifeline and heart are quite explicit. Another North American example is seen in plate 60.

13. **Bulls superimposed on an aurochs.** *c*. 15,000–12,000 BC. Cave painting. l. (of bull) *c*. 13 ft. 1½ in. (4 m.). Lascaux, France. The Lascaux bulls are not as fully modelled as the Altamira ones, but they give a more spirited impression. The repeated use of an area of rock for new pictures as occasion arose is well illustrated in the lower part and the top right of this plate.

14 (opposite). **The 'Venus of Laussel'.** *c*. 15,000–10,000 BC. Rock relief carving. h. 18 in. (46 cm.). Musée d'Aquitaine, Bordeaux. This powerful image is one of the earliest stone sculptures of the female nude in the history of world art. Classical conceptions of ideal human beauty are no help in approaching its significance and peculiarities, nor can its unflinching naturalism in the portrayal of gross physical features be put down to faithfulness to appearances, for the head and hands are perfunctory. The distended flesh and pendulous breasts represent a generalised type of childbearing woman, and stress fertility. As with the ivory figurines of 'Venuses' from Willendorf and elsewhere, the personal details of the face and hands were felt to be unimportant. The (blood-filled) horn she is holding is connected with myths of the 'mistress of the beasts', a kind of goddess who holds sway over animals and drives them toward the hunters.

15, 16. Woollen carpet from Grave V, Pazyryk, Siberia (details). *c.* 500 BC. l. (of whole carpet) 11 ft. 6 in. (350 cm.). State Hermitage Museum, Leningrad. As with the Pueblo Indian bowl (plate 12), the decoration of this very ancient oriental carpet—the oldest in the world—combines naturalistic motifs of an early type (16) with the abstract motifs (15) which evolved from them. The knotting and design tell us that the carpet was manufactured in Iran or the Caucasus.

17 (opposite). Buddha in meditation. Tibetan *tanka* painting. h. *c.* 20 in. (50 cm.). Rietberg Museum, Zürich. The subjects and their forms come mainly from Indian art, but the whirling lines emanating from the Buddha's solar plexus are a Tibetan peculiarity and go back to the ideas of the prehistoric hunters. This *tanka* (temple banner) illustrates the Tibetan Buddhist belief, rooted in the trance-inducing practices of Central Asian shamanism, that if a mystic's contemplation is intense enough, initiates can see the 'energy-currents' of his body *(prana)* taking shape as radiating ripples of air.

18, 19. The 'Leopard Dancers' from Çatal Hüyük, S. Anatolia (Turkey) (details). *c.* 6000 BC. Wall painting. Archaeological Museum, Ankara. Only unearthed in 1961, this is an exciting record of humanity's major step forward with the coming into being of the first true towns in southern Anatolia. These are the earliest known paintings that were not made on natural rock but on the plaster-washed walls of houses. (The fragment in plate 19 is about 3 ft in length). The appearance of animated naturalistic human figures reflected the shift of interest away from animals of the chase. It profoundly influenced people still leading a hunter existence in the western Mediterranean, whose animals-and-humans style eventually spread through Africa (plates 87, 89, 92). The leaping, spinning figures with dotted bands spreading out round them probably represent dancers clad in leopard skins. If so, we may have the earliest pictures of the ecstatic rites of the cult of Dionysos, which the Greeks said originated in Asia Minor.

20 (opposite). **Early Chinese tiger's head,** Chou dynasty. *c.* 1027–221 BC. Bronze inlaid with silver. l. 2¾ in. (7 cm.). Museum für Ostasiatische Kunst, Cologne. This little masterpiece of early Chinese metalwork illustrates the shamanist-inspired animal style from Central Asia elegantly clothed in a late Chou abstract decoration based on the spiral motif. The handling of volume in the small scale of the bronze head is impressive and the application of the hammered inlay is highly accomplished.

the so-called 'X-ray style', the full face lion, and the animal glancing backwards.

A brief outline of the so-called X-ray style will throw light on the outlook of the early hunters and on such vestiges of this as have survived to the present day. The term is used to denote a style that for magical purposes depicts on the outside of the prey internal organs which the hunter well knows are vital. Frequently they are simplified as a 'life line' reaching from the animal's mouth to its heart or stomach. The earliest traces of the X-ray style are not encountered in rock pictures, but in incised bone fragments from south-western France, dating from the late Magdalenian period, somewhere between 13,000 and 6000 BC. There is one painting of an earlier epoch which has some claim to be regarded as belonging to the X-ray style. It is an Ice Age mammoth in the Pindal cave in northern Spain with a big red patch probably representing the heart, painted inside the outline.

It is curious that the X-ray style does not seem to have spread from its place of origin to any other part of Spain or to northern Africa. Instead, it spreads continuously northward and eastward, finally to North America by way of Siberia, and to Australia. The rock pictures most closely comparable with figures in the distinctive X-ray style are to be found in the Arctic art of Norway (6000–2000 BC). There is no doubt that these Arctic pictures are related to the Magdalenian works of south-western France, but the question of how this style reached Norway is still a vexed one. It may have spread to Russia and reached Norway from there. The rock pictures of northern Russia and Siberia bear a great resemblance to those of Norway, especially to those in the eastern group, and almost identical renderings can be found at the two extreme points within the area in which Arctic art spread: Norway on the Atlantic and the Amur-Ussuri region on the Pacific. A late continuation of the X-ray style is to be found on the painted drumskins used until quite recent times by the shamans of Lapland.

In the rock engravings of central Norway, the internal organs have been reduced to a pattern of rectangles and lozenges, and this process of abstraction can be seen with wonderful clarity in a single rock picture group *in situ* at Skogerveien, Buskerud. It includes several stages of reduction from the literal depiction of the vital organs by circles linked by a life line with the animal's mouth to a mere criss-cross of lines.

There was another motif which evolved in south western France: a beast, usually a lion, with its face turned towards the viewer. This motif appears for the first time in the caves at Trois Frères in the Pyrenees, spreads through northern Africa, and survives in Benin bronzes of the sixteenth century AD, and even in the minor arts of West Africa at the present day.

It is curious that the motif of the full-face beast, in contrast to the X-ray style, spread not northward but only southward and eastward from the Franco-Cantabrian area. This suggests that out of the common fund of basic hunter motifs some must have crystallised at an early stage and failed to penetrate into areas where some other concept was dominant. The full-face lion motif was connected with the idea of the evil eye in beasts of prey, whereas the X-ray style was connected with the belief in reanimation-magic from the pieces of a dead animal, which is the origin of shamanism.

The German anthropologist, Leo Frobenius (1873–1938), who pioneered the world-wide copying and collection of all extant rock pictures for comparison on the widest possible basis, made some significant deductions from the motif of the animal glancing backward:

> Wherever we encounter this motif in early western art the animals give the impression, not only of 'glancing backward', but also of being startled and beginning to flee. True, in the first picture from the Ariège the fleeing bull is shown pursued by a figure; but this does not take us very far towards an explanation, for this representation is the mysterious figure of what appears to be a masked man. We are left with the question: fleeing from whom? The answer is provided by finds excavated at Susa and Nineveh, which show the same motif persisting strongly in western Asia from early times.

The earlier designs, familiar from the ceramic ware of Susa (Period II), are rather primitive. One shows a bird of prey flying at the throat of an animal with its head turned backward. This design occurs again on carved shell discs in Mesopotamia, and it is interesting that the attacking bird's beak already bears little resemblance to that of a bird of prey, and a quadruped also appears in this role in Susa II, but with little that is savage about it. By the time of the Tello site (2100 BC), it has become a lion, and the motif grew increasingly monumental in the art of western Asia until it culminated in the massive and static figures that ornamented the palace of Darius at Persepolis. It had thus kept it potency for many centuries. Frobenius remarks:

> All these bowls—from Susa I, by way of Nineveh, down to the Etruscan period—bear cosmological pictures. The animals move along the horizon of the ocean as though

21 (opposite). **Early Chinese sacral vessel** *(yu)*. Shang dynasty. *c.* 1500–1027 BC. Cast bronze. h. 14 in. (35.5 cm.). Musée Cernuschi, Paris. The outlook of shamanism could hardly be more graphically expressed than by this superb early Chinese bronze ritual wine vessel *(yu)*. The small figure of a man is *not* being devoured by the tiger, he is clinging to his tutelary tiger-spirit for protection. The great paws hold the man gently as he shelters under the tiger's fangs. The rich surface decoration consists in part of stylised dragons on the tiger and stylised snakes on the man. The same conception appears in ancient America, where men are often portrayed looking out of animal or bird helmets (plate 46) or skins. Man and his guardian spirit are seen as two natures combined in one image.

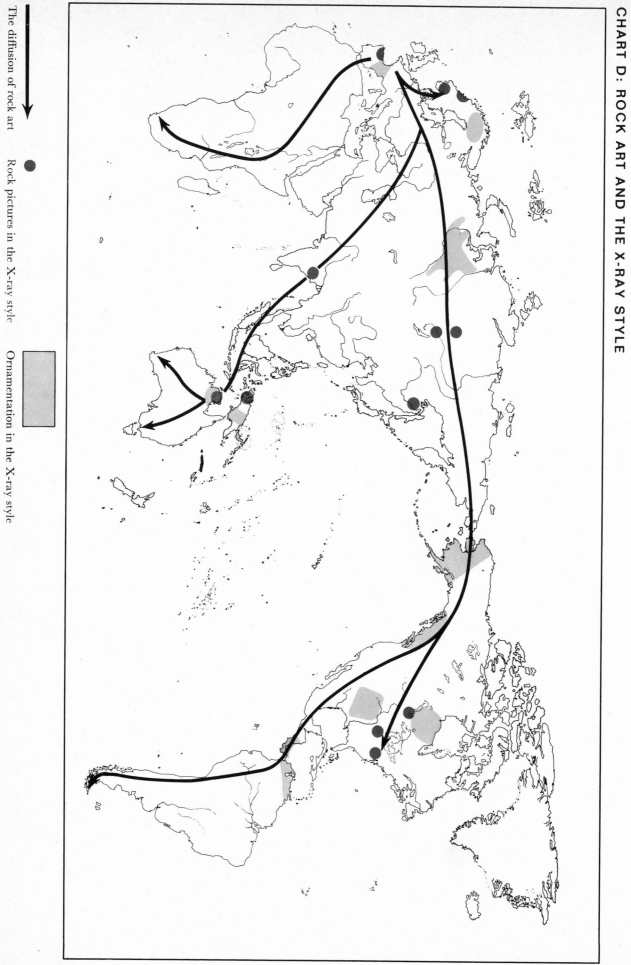

CHART D: ROCK ART AND THE X-RAY STYLE

The diffusion of rock art

● Rock pictures in the X-ray style

Ornamentation in the X-ray style

10. **Arctic art rock painting of elks and various symbols**
c. 5000–2000 BC. l. (of groups) 9 ft. 6 in. (280 cm.) Hinna,
Møre og Romsdal, Norway (central group). Painted in red·
beneath an overhanging cliff, these middle-period Arctic rock
pictures show a tendency toward stylisation. A drawing of a
detail from the left half is seen in figure 7*c*.

they were stars in heaven. It seems as though in a later period a final and generally comprehensible definition was found for what at the dawning of the human consciousness could only be expressed 'mutely'.

Our increasing knowledge of the origins of western Asiatic civilisation and art makes it appear quite natural in mythological terms for animal heads to be adorned with constellations and star-symbols. The bull bears the symbol of its lunar nature, denoting the onset of darkness, just as the sun in the guise of a lion dispels the moon and stars each morning—the sun-lion is flying at the throat of the moon-bull. The myths of the mature cultures of the Middle East in this way illuminate the meaning of the far earlier Stone Age art of the West. Researchers in this field might well be invited to consider whether an allegorical sameness was felt by the Mesopotamians to exist between the majestic and terrible sight of a lion's glance in real life, when it could mean instant death to the hunter, and the equally terrible sun, whose mighty morning rays obliterated the stars of the night, and conversely between the unnumbered herds of beasts of the chase and the stars that the sun drove from the heavens.

Symbolic language of this kind could certainly be reconciled with what Frobenius learned about a now extinct hunting culture in the Sahara, called 'Mahalbi'. He was able to witness hunting magic being practised by the members of one of the last groups belonging to this culture before all of them had died out. These hunters believed that all animals they hunted were sent to them by an animal deity, which appeared to them in animal form more often than in human form. They called this deity the 'lord of animals' or 'buffalo father', and their prayer to him was the ritual which Frobenius saw: they made sketches of the animals in the sand and, at the moment of the rising sun, sprinkled them from a horn full of blood. This idea of a horn filled with blood which the 'buffalo father' had given to the people played an important part in the Mahalbi rites and we can assume that similar ideas are the background to the horn held in the right hand of the woman in the Magdalenian rock relief called the 'Venus of Laussel'.

Where concepts of this type are found to occur, the 'buffalo father' is sometimes thought of as having originally corresponded to the moon. It is conceivable that when Stone Age people drew or engraved the images of animals on the walls deep in their underground shrines—for this was undoubtedly the purpose of their caves—they were in their mind's eye a metaphor for the celestial strife of the stars, the moon and the sun.

The last survival of original European hunter art was among the Lapps of northern Scandinavia, down to the seventeenth century. Some most interesting comparisons can be made between prehistoric rock pictures and Lapp art, particularly in the painted shaman drums of which a great many are now in museums. These drums are not only the shaman's indispensable instrument for inducing the trance which is central to his magic rites, but are works of

art in their own right. Shaman drums from Lapland and Siberia are painted on the skin with representational designs which do not depend on a random choice but are significant illustrations of the hunter-artists' cosmology. Lapp drumskins often have a lozenge in the centre, from which four rays divide the surface into sectors. The lozenge stands for the sun and the other figures, which may be of humans, animals or objects, all have a bearing on the shamanist world-picture. They include the gods of thunder, of the wind and of the nether world, together with others that refer to the life and breeding of reindeer and other animals. Camps, settlements, graves and the nether world were also depicted.

Although the appearance of the deities and of the nether world have been influenced by the later Nordic-Germanic inhabitants of Scandinavia, and although Christian elements also occur in a simplified form, some very ancient concepts and motifs seem to have been preserved on these drums, such as renderings of animals in the X-ray style and possibly the use of a motif comparable to the 'trap' symbol of the Magdalenian cave artists which is discussed on page 44. The rare use of the X-ray rendering connects Lapp art with that of the Arctic hunters who produced rock paintings in Southern Sweden and Norway between 6000 and 2000 BC. This does not mean that the Lapps themselves were living in Scandinavia during this early period (they probably arrived later from the north-east), but it is evident that they have preserved the forms of an ancient hunter culture which must have flourished in southern Scandinavia before the entry of the Germanic peoples into this area from the south-east.

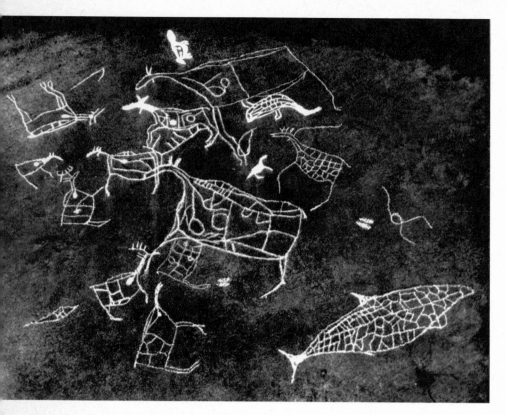

11. **Rock engraving of stylised animals and a whale,** drawn over with chalk. Arctic art (eastern group), *c.* 5000–2000 BC. l. (of whale), 4 ft. 7 in. (140 cm.). Skogerveien, Drammen, Buskerud, Norway. 'Arctic art' is the term applied to clearly-defined groups of Stone Age rock pictures distributed over Scandinavia and northern Russia. They were produced by hunters and fishermen still living as the people of the Aurignacian and Magdalenian periods had done at the end of the Ice Age. The earlier Arctic art rock pictures, in northern Norway (see figure 4), are the most naturalistic and are clearly linked with late Aurignacian art in western Europe, though probably by an eastern route. In the later phases, the X-ray style became increasingly stylised, as can be seen in this photograph.

The stylised life-line which the Lapps draw on the reindeer that decorate the shaman drums is a vestige of the X-ray style, and is connected with their concept of *saivo.* This is an abode of animal spirits, not a nether world of the dead. It is a widespread idea among the primitive people of northern Eurasia that a hunting expedition will succeed if the souls of the animals that are to be caught have first been subjugated with the aid of a shaman. They are drawn with their vital organs visible, so that they may attain reincarnation. It was thought that a slain animal could be resurrected from its bones, hide and the like. The X-ray style is a manifestation of these ideas, which are basic both to shamanism and the early hunter culture, and it is found solely in areas inhabited by hunters.

The fine and representative specimen of a shaman drum which is reproduced opposite illustrates the world of *saivo.* The drawing on the drum skin in this case is divided not into four sectors, which would be more usual, but into three horizontal registers. The top one contains either two suns or a sun and a moon, with a tent, deities, the heavens and the upper world. The middle register portrays a world of the dead, and the lowest register shows another nether world in which there are the figures of three *akkas,* or goddesses of the underworld. In the middle register on the left is a female figure surrounded by animals. This is the mistress of the beasts, who 'sends' their souls to the hunters. Next to her is a reindeer with a hint of the X-ray style, and a hunter who is trying to slay it with an arrow. This is probably the shaman who has descended into this spiritual nether world, the world of dreams, in order to persuade the

animals' souls to cede their bodies to the hunters. On the right-hand side, running upwards, there is a human figure in a sleigh drawn by a harnessed reindeer, also marked with the hint of a life line, followed by a dog. Here we doubtless see the shaman on his way to rejoin the world above. The dog may be creature of the nether world that is trying to prevent him from leaving.

We have seen here how two elements in works of art from a later period help to elucidate the meaning of certain symbols or abstract geometric patterns in the otherwise naturalistic rock pictures of the Magdalenian period. In the Lascaux paintings, for example, there are unexplained rectangles with transverse bars or lattices in them, close to some paintings of wild cattle. These designs are often referred to as 'traps'. Sometimes the lattice covers the whole animal, so that it looks as if it is in a cage. It is, however, unlikely that these represent traps in our sense of the word, and are more probably symbols which were used in hunting magic rules and intended to catch the soul of the animals to be hunted—they were, in all probability, a hunting instrument on the psychic rather than the physical plane. They may also indicate some kind of erasure, whereby a naturalistic picture is 'killed' by drawing lines across it. It may also serve to emphasise the ghostly content of the picture.

The evidences that we thus find in the shamanism of recent times not only furnishes us with the means of interpreting the motifs of rock paintings, but of establishing a whole system of styles as well. It is therefore significant to find that these are to be found on a rock picture in southern

12. **Figures on the skin of a Lapp
drum from northern Sweden.** *c.* 1800.
diameter *c.* 14½ in. (37 cm.). Museum für
Völkerkunde, Munich. The images
painted on the drums of the Lapp
shamans are an important source of our
knowledge of the mental world of
shamanism. A drum was an essential part
of a shaman's equipment. With it he beat
out the rhythm that helped to induce the
trance in which he brought his psychic
powers to bear for the good of the
community. The back of this specimen,
the significance of which is discussed on
the opposite page, is enclosed with a
hemispherical body carved out of a single
piece of wood.

Sweden belonging to the Arctic period, in addition to animals in X-ray style, also geometric designs—sharp-angled lozenges, singly and in chains. This gives us the association of a more or less naturalistic with an entirely geometric style in Palaeolithic rock paintings (from about 20,000 BC), in Arctic rock pictures (6000–2000 BC) and in Australian rock pictures of this century.

Between 9000 and 8000 BC there was a comparatively rapid change of climate. The ice receded and the frozen plains, or tundra, where herds of game had formerly wandered, became covered by large forests. Many species retreated northward or died out, while the forests provided shelter for multitudes of the wild animals that would be familiar to modern man. The rain belt also shifted northward, leaving other areas in northern Africa and south-western Asia to become arid. Their inhabitants were forced to seek more fertile lands to live in. In a climate basically like our own, though probably slightly warmer, the Old Stone Age (Palaeolithic) came to an end and a transitional stage developed. This is called the Mesolithic, and gradually led to the beginnings of agriculture. The hunters continued to exist, using for the most part the same tools as before, but with rather more attention to working bone and horn. A culture known as the 'Maglemosian' (named after the Danish word, *maglemose*, meaning a bog) with fishing as an important extension of the hunter's means of livelihood, came into being about 7500 BC, stretching from East Anglia to north-western Russia. Man became familiar with the use of fish-hooks, nets, harpoons and paddles. Dug-outs were probably in use. The art of this people consisted of animal figurines carved in amber and of occasional engravings on bone.

THE CLUE OF THE HARPOON

The harpoon serves as an example to illustrate the gradual diffusion of the hunters over the whole world. This ingenious weapon first appears at Roland Bay in southern France during the final stage of the Upper Palaeolithic, in the Magdalenian period (15,000 -10,000 BC). The next site, dating from about 1200 BC, is Stellmoor near Ahrensburg, not far from Hamburg. The harpoon spread from Europe through Russia to Siberia, where it has been authenticated at Serovo on the river Angara (about 3000 BC). From Siberia it found its way into China between about 2500 and 1500 BC. One find in Manchuria has been dated to 5000 BC, but this is an exception and seems too early in relation to the evidence for the occurrence of harpoons in the rest of eastern Asia. The harpoon was widely diffused in Neolithic Japan by about 1000 BC, and reached Formosa at about the same time. The early occurrence of harpoons in Siberia may explain the fact that they are still being used today on the shores of inland seas and lakes in Russian Central Asia (the Caspian and Aral Seas, lakes Issyk-Kul and Zaysan).

In Africa, harpoons have been found in large quantities along the lower Nile (Fayum, from 4200 BC) and along its upper reaches (near Khartum, from 3000 BC). Comparable sites from the same period extend all through the Sudan to West Africa, on the upper Nile among the Nuer people, on the shores of the great lakes, and along the Congo, and may be associated with the dissemination of harpoons during the Neolithic era. In Alaska the weapon occurs about the time of Christ in the Old Bering culture, which developed on the Asiatic side of the Bering Strait. It survives to the present day in the Arctic districts of eastern Siberia, among the Eskimos and the Aleuts, and has reached Greenland and Labrador. Beaten copper harpoons of the early copper culture already occur about 1000 BC around the Great Lakes, and bone harpoons are found in North American mounds of various types dating from the first to the seventeenth centuries AD. In South America the harpoon is encountered sporadically in the Guyanas, the Amazon region, ancient Peru and Tierra del Fuego. On the basis of comparative studies, Oswald Menghin claims to have traced a single type of basic harpoon from Ahrensburg, *via* northern California, to South America, where he dates its arrival to about 2000 BC at the latest.

In India the harpoon appears in the 'copper hoards' about 700 BC. It is present in Bronze Age finds in Indochina dating from about 300 BC and occurs repeatedly among small groups of fishermen living along the coast of Burma, in the Mergui archipelago, the Andaman and Nicobar islands and in eastern Indonesia. Around the Pacific Ocean, the harpoon has survived among the Ainu in northern Japan and the Haida Indians in north-western America. In the Marquesas islands it was in use before the arrival of the Europeans. It has been found by archaeologists on both North Island and South Island in New Zealand, as well as in the Chatham Islands. The last place it reached, where only faint traces remain, was southern New Guinea and northern Australia. It was known in the Torres Strait area and, as rock paintings testify, must have also reached north-eastern Arnhem Land and the northernmost part of Cape York Peninsula, as well as Groote Eylandt in the Gulf of Carpentaria.

The harpoons found in the Marquesas, New Zealand and the Chatham Islands are obviously akin to those used by fishermen in the Arctic. Those from the Torres Strait have more affinity with similar implements in India. (Only the rock pictures of harpoons in northern Australia cannot be classified for certain either as to age or origin.) The fact that harpoons were fashioned identically in areas located at immense distances from one another is not only proof of early migration by groups of hunters but proof that this implement originated in western Europe during the Magdalenian period. The earlier forms of culture among hunters the world over must have come into being in western Europe and spread elsewhere without undergoing any major change. Both the implements and the way of life remained constant.

13. **Rock engraving of a fawn.** Palaeolithic. Grotta di Levanzo, Aegadian islands, west of Sicily.

14. **Bronze plaque of a stag.** Ordos Steppe, Inner Mongolia. h. 2 in. (5 cm.). Museum für Völkerkunde, Munich. The motif of an animal with its head turned backward. The exquisite reduction of form in figure 14 is reminiscent of Japanese craftsmanship, which may have been influenced by the Ordos style *via* China.

22. Drum-stand in the form of cranes and snakes from Ch'ang-sha, China. Chou dynasty. *c.* 1027–221 BC. Lacquered wood. h. 4 ft. 3¾ in. (131.5 cm.). J. H. Wade Collection, Museum of Art, Cleveland. Snakes were a feature of the Huai style, which represented the peak of mounted-nomad influence in Chinese art. They were regarded as promoters of fertility, and served as models for the Chinese dragon when it acquired its final form. In this piece the two cranes represent the upper world and the two snakes joined in copulation at their feet symbolise the earth and its fruitfulness. The slender lines of the figures and the positive-negative surface pattern anticipate the typical style of Indonesia. The bird-snake motif was to occur plentifully in Indonesia as well as in India and Melanesia.

23. **Ornament with spirals and animal heads from northern China.**
5th–2nd centuries BC. Bronze. h. 2 in. (5 cm.). Museum für Völkerkunde, Munich. A clear example of the combination of parts of animals (perhaps wolves' heads?) with the pure spiral form as their bodies. It was an old hunter-peoples belief, expressed here in the Siberian 'dismembered' style, that even the pieces of an animal gave the shaman power to resuscitate a whole one in its place.

24. **Chinese bronze mask.** Han
dynasty. 200 BC–220 AD. h. 2¼ in.
(5.7 cm.). Museum für Völkerkunde,
Munich. Miniature decorative masks like
this were attached to clothing or
accoutrements to signify a tiger-spirit's
protection for the wearer. This totemistic
idea is illustrated in plate 21. The strong
design unites naturalism with bold
spiral forms.

25. **Bronze ornament from the Ordos region, northern China.** 5th–2nd centuries BC. h. 1½ in. (4 cm.). Museum für Völkerkunde, Munich. A typical open-work bronze plaque from the Ordos region (charts E, G), where numerous pieces of this kind have been found. The motif of animals 'stacked' one above the other—in this example, they seem to be horses with bushy manes between the ears—may have had a fertility-promoting significance. It spread from N.-W. China right through Indonesia.

26 (opposite). **Ikat textile from Sumba Island, Indonesia.** Late 19th century. Woven cotton. h. 3 ft. 10 in. (117 cm.). Museum für Völkerkunde, Munich. Although it was made in modern times, the stags, snakes and dolphins as well as the abstract patterns on this cotton tapestry recall Chinese motifs of the Han period (c. 200 BC–200 AD). These forms were preserved more distinctly on Sumba then elsewhere in Indonesia. The fabrics were used as festive cloaks by the living and as shrouds for the dead. The design was first painted on the warp, and the weft had to follow it exactly. The 'skull-trees' between the stags should be noted: they used to be found at the entry to every village and on them the skulls of slain enemies would be displayed as a protection against evil spirits.

54

27 (below). **Head of a unicorn from northern China.** 2nd century BC. Early Han dynasty (206 BC–220 AD). Bronze. h. 2¾ in. (7 cm.). Museum für Völkerkunde, Munich. The treatment of the head remains quite naturalistic even when the animal itself is probably a fabulous one introduced into China along with the mounted nomad animal style. The vivid green patina is due to long burial in the soil.

28 (opposite, above). **Chinese bronze belt clasp.** Early Han dynasty (206 BC–220 AD). Bronze inlaid with gold. l. 6¾ in. (17 cm.). Museum für Völkerkunde, Munich. Long-tongued belt clasps became fashionable in late Chou and early Han times (3rd–2nd century BC), doubtless borrowed from the mounted nomads. They were a feature of knightly trappings during the decline of Chinese feudalism. The gold-inlaid dragon's head (far right) is naturalistic, but the body tails off in spiral motifs. The scroll-like forms have affinities with Bronze Age art in Europe.

29 (opposite, below). **Batak textile, Sumatra** (detail). 19th–20th century. Woven cotton. h. (of complete textile) 23¾ in. (60 cm.). Museum für Völkerkunde, Munich. Textiles like this were still being woven at the beginning of the 20th century and preserved—as in the band below the border—the ancient spiral motifs in a geometric form. The pattern here is typical of Sumatra and, to a lesser extent, of Borneo.

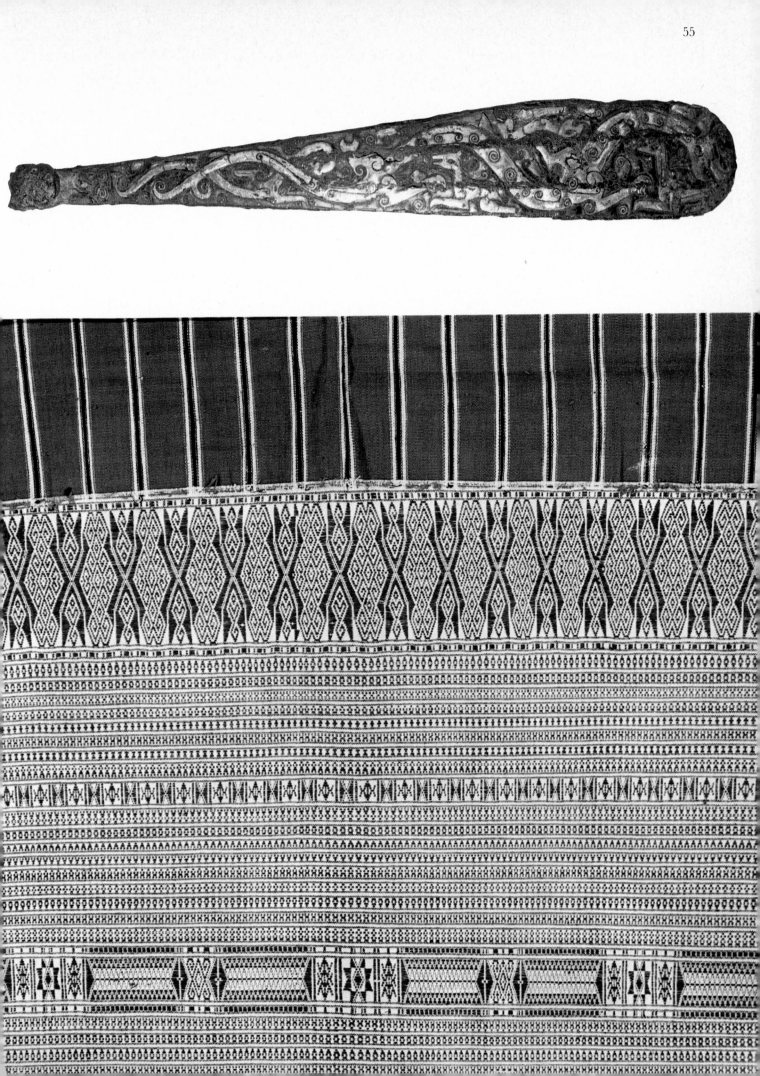

30 (below). **Painted jar from Ning-ting-hsien,** Kansu, China. 2nd millennium BC. Pottery. h. 13¾ in. (35 cm.). Museum für Völkerkunde, Munich.

32 (opposite, below). **Incised pottery bowl** (underside) from Sepik valley, New Guinea. 19th–20th century. Diameter 11¾ in. (30 cm.). Museum für Völker-kunde, Munich. The persistence of the spiral motif is shown in these two pottery vessels. The Neolithic Chinese jar (known as Pan Shan ware) was already decorated with a derivative of the spiral, the original of which can be traced back to early farming cultures in western Russia, c. 3000 BC (though some Chinese scholars are reluctant to admit any 'foreign' sources for their art). The New Guinea bowl, of recent make, still uses fully developed spirals in a vigorous design which is also found carved in wood or bone.

31. Ornament of carved jade
(nephrite). North Island, New Zealand,
19th century. l. 1¾ in. (4.5 cm.). Museum
für Völkerkunde, Munich. The art of the
Polynesians, to whose race the Maoris
belong, reached a high degree of
sophisticated stylisation in New Zealand,
especially in carved and polished
'greenstone' ornaments and pendants.
This fish abstracted to a spiral form and
the ancestor figure *hei tiki* (plate 37)
enshrine two basic motifs of the farming
peoples of Oceania.

33. Axe from the Solomon Islands, Melanesia. Early 20th century. Greenstone. l. 16½ in. (42 cm.). **Gourd flask from New Caledonia, Melanesia.** Early 20th century. h. 12½ in. (32 cm.). Both subjects, Museum für Völkerkunde, Munich.

34 (opposite, above). **Olmec celts from El Mangal,** Vera Cruz State, Mexico. *c.* 1500 AD. Diopside-jadeite. l. 11 and 8½ in. (28.2 and 21.5 cm.). Robert Woods Bliss Collection, National Gallery of Art, Washington. Finds of these typical polished stone axes with an oval section

enable us to trace the migrations of the early farmers in S.-E. Asia and Oceania. The Olmec ceremonial celts are proofs of their strong influence in Central America. The modern Melanesian utensils have changed little since the Neolithic era (2nd millennium BC).

35. **Fabric with boats design from the Kroë region,** S. Sumatra. 20th century. Cotton. l. 9 ft. 2¼ in. (280 cm.). Museum für Völkerkunde, Munich. Boats are a frequent subject in Indonesian art, where they have a double meaning. They represent the migration of the ancestors of the tribe by sea; as they refer to ancestral events, they therefore also symbolise the 'world beyond'. The spiral motif pervades the design in every part of the fabric.

36. **Head of a Batak sorcerer's carved staff,** Sumatra. Probably 19th century. Wood and feathers. British Museum, London. The Batak 'magic wands' are full of interest from several points of view. Between 5 and 6 feet in height, they were carried by sorcerers both as a personal attribute and as a symbol of the accumulated power of the ancestors whose figures are crouched round the shaft. The Bataks were keen horsemen (see chart E) and the uppermost figure was often, as here, depicted as one.

37 (opposite). **Hei tiki pendant from New Zealand.** 19th century. Jade (nephrite) with inlaid mother-of-pearl. h. 5 in. (12.5 cm.). Museum für Völkerkunde, Munich. Maori chieftains wore these well-known pendants which are a stylised form of squatting figure—probably the deified ancestor of the Polynesians, Tiki. The tilted head also connects it with the idea of an embryo before birth. The enlargement reveals the marks of work with stones and abrasives. Metal was unknown, and these were all the Maoris had for cutting and polishing the hard jade into shape.

38. **Ancestor figure from the Babar Islands,** Indonesia. 19th century. Wood. h. 4 ft. 8¾ in. (144 cm.). Museum für Völkerkunde, Munich. Here and in figure 54 we see the distinct prototype all the squatting ancestor figures in eastern Indonesia and beyond. Figures like these were carved in wood on the Babar Islands until recent times, though the example shown here in colour is probably of considerable age. The floral design in relief on the base may be a sign of Islamic influence from western Indonesia.

39 (opposite). **Bagobo textile from Mindanao,** Philippines. (detail). 19th century. Cotton and abaca fibres. l. (of whole textile) 5 ft. 9¼ in. (176 cm.). Museum für Völkerkunde, Munich. Very stylised ancestor figures in squatting postures appear in the broad vertical band, closely resembling the ambiguous figures of men and frogs on Neolithic Yang Shao pottery from China. An unborn human is even shown in the body of a frog-ancestor. The rest of the design is based on spirals. A plant fibre weft on the cotton warp means that this is an antique piece. The abaca plant, relative of the banana tree, produces a sort of Manila hemp, still used for making ropes and matting.

Agriculture requires a completely different relationship between man and his environment. His interest in game and the procreation of animals gradually lessens and he becomes more and more preoccupied with the fertility of the soil on which he depends for his livelihood. An entirely new kind of symbolism in art develops from this new relationship. The snake is the symbol of the soil, and it is snake motifs, with their phallic associations, which frequently predominate in art all the way from Mesopotamia, where they originate, to India, China and Central America.

The period that begins with the discovery of food production is called the Neolithic or New Stone Age. It is also the period in which pottery was invented. Pottery began in Anatolia in the early Neolithic era, between about 7000 and 6000 BC, when the first clay ware came into use alongside hollowed-out stone vessels. At first it was produced by simply pressing lumps of clay into the required shape by hand, yet even long before the invention of the potter's wheel men were already capable of giving their pottery vessels aesthetically satisfying forms with polished surfaces that invited painted decoration. Painted pottery dates from the late Neolithic era (about 6500–5500 BC) in southern Anatolia.

With the appearance of pottery and of various kinds of decoration on it in the sites of ancient human settlements, archaeologists find their earliest reliable means of defining specific cultures and tracing their diffusion. The original home of the potter's wheel is still unknown, but it was being used in Egypt and India from the middle of the third millennium BC onward, and it reached China not much later. It never got to America in pre-Columbian times, and the exquisitely finished ceramics of Peru continued to be made entirely without the help of the potter's wheel until the Spanish conquest in the sixteenth century AD.

The earliest form of decoration on this new, important and durable vehicle consisted of circular and spiral designs. By 4000 BC, these abstract designs were blended with naturalistic figures of animals, usually stags and mountain goats such as have been found at Siyalk in Iran. One of the earliest of such combinations was produced at Samarra in northern Iraq between 5500 and 5000 BC, and this style exerted an influence as far afield as Harappa, one

30
56

18 (above). **Late Neolithic polychrome painted vessel from Thessaly.** *c.* 2500 BC. White pottery painted with black and red. Dimini, near Volos, Greece. National Museum, Athens.

19 (below). **Danubian Neolithic flask** from the cult cave called Jungfernhöhle in Franconia. *c.* 3000 BC. Incised ware. h. 5⅝ in. (14.3 cm.). Prähistorische Staatssammlung, Munich. As the art of decorated pottery spread into Europe from the centres of mature culture in western Asia, it carried with it motifs of Middle Eastern origin, such as the spiral (above), one of the symbols of the farming peoples' fertility cults.

40 (opposite). **Peruvian textile from a tomb.** *c.* 1000 AD. Llama wool. h. (of whole textile) 9 ft. 6 in. (291 cm.). Museum für Völkerkunde, Munich. The presence of the spiral motif in ancient America is documented three times in the weaving of this piece. The distinctive 'step and fret' motif of the lower part, which appears in the masonry of countless Mexican and Andean monuments, is a geometrical variant of the spiral. An earlier, rounded form of spiral meander runs along the strips enclosing the border, the interior of which consists of another geometrical variant. The boldly coloured but static design is wholly pre-Columbian in feeling.

Female fertility figures of the Neolithic farmers in Europe, *c.* 2000–1500 BC.

20. **Baked clay figurine from Tatar Pazardjik,** near Plovdiv, Bulgaria. h. 3½ in. (9.5 cm.). Naturhistorisches Museum, Vienna.

21. **Baked and painted clay figurines from Střelice,** Znojmo district, Moravia, Czechoslovakia. h. (l. to r.) 8¼ in. (21 cm.), 8½ in. (22 cm.). Moravian Museum, Brno.

22. **Baked and incised clay female idol from Cyprus.** Louvre, Paris.

23. **Carved marble 'Cycladic' figure.** National Museum, Athens. To the primitive artist, the female body is not an object to be represented for its own sake, but an ever-present symbol of the desperately important powers of growth and multiplication. So the figure of the 'great mother', who ensured the fertility of animals, plants and mankind, became a symbol of life and rebirth. From the earliest Aurignacian examples (plate 14), artists making these cult-images concentrated on the physical aspects which emphasise female sexuality, and tended to turn these into abstract forms which are themselves aesthetically satisfying.

of the great sites of the Indus valley civilisation. In pre-dynastic Egypt, the prominently painted spirals on the pottery of the Gerzean culture (about 3400 BC) show the strong influence of this style reaching in the other direction. When the spiral first came into use in the Middle East it can be assumed that its meaning was symbolic of the earth (the snake-emblem), of life and of the idea of eternal renewal. This meaning tended to be left behind when the spiral spread eastward and westward as a ready-made decorative motif and nothing more. Its further progress across Asia and America is described on pages 72–3 and 135–40.

THE FIRST CITIES IN THE WORLD

Just as agriculture and the domestication of animals had been discovered in western Asia, so also was the step from village to town life taken there, the step from a primitive to an advanced organisation of society. The latest excavations at Çatal Hüyük in southern Anatolia and at Jericho have brought to light walled and fortified urban settlements which came into being about 6000 BC. The chief civilisations of the ancient Middle East have their origin several thousand years later. The beginnings of Sumer were about 3500 BC, and the beginnings of Egypt were about 3200 BC. It was another thousand years before urban civilisation appeared in China (about 1500 BC) and in the Indus Valley (about 2500 BC).

The mature cultures in the Middle East and China drastically altered the status of the primitive cultures and their subsequent development. (The Indus Valley civilisation collapsed around 1500 BC, but not before it had its effect on the primitive cultures of India, as a comparison of primitive village art in India of even recent times with Indus Valley art can show.) Until this time, the advance of humanity had been the work of primitive communities. Now they became outsiders. The future lay with the new mature cultures which embodied and carried forward the ideas and achievements of the hunters and farmers. These inherited elements gained definite and recognisable forms.

From this point onward, progress came to mean only one thing: integration in their own traditions of as much as they could of what the mature cultures had to offer. They had to find a way of preserving what was valuable in their own heritage while assimilating the often overpowering influence of the mature culture. The effect of China on the surrounding peoples has already been mentioned (page 10). It was the same for the Dravidian tribes of central and southern India after the rise of Hindu civilisation in the northern plains.

The influence of the Middle East was felt throughout the Mediterranean, in North Africa and northern Europe. An example of its influence penetrating to northern Asia is found in the introduction into shamanism of Persian ideas of dualism—the conflict of good and evil forces in the universe—which was entirely lacking in the beliefs of original shamanism. During the Chou dynasty (first millennium BC), China experienced various cultural

The megalithic style in Europe
24 (above). **Temple at Hagar Qim, Malta.** *c.* 2000 BC.
25 (below). **Stonehenge from the air.** Between *c.* 1900 and 1600 BC. A powerful new religion, centered on worship of the 'great mother', spread from the eastern Mediterranean to N.-W. Europe between 3000 and 2000 BC. Shrines and tombs built with huge blocks of stone, the walls and uprights often topped by massive lintels (above, below), were its characteristic style. In Stonehenge each significant stone aligns with at least one other to point to some extreme position of the sun or moon.

26 (below). **Incised spirals from New Grange, Ireland** (in the north recess of the barrow tomb). *c.* 2000 BC. The megalithic builders of the tombs in the Boyne valley near Dublin used the spiral motif profusely on the lining slabs.

27. **Bronze cult chariot from Strettweg,** Styria. Hallstatt culture. Landesmuseum Joanneum, Graz. The antlered stags and the armed horsemen show the pervasive influence of the style of the mounted nomads of the Eurasian plains, even in this graceful and expressive Iron Age group from Central Europe.

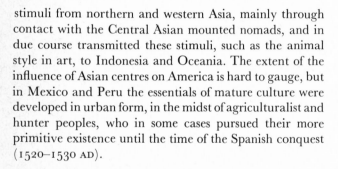

stimuli from northern and western Asia, mainly through contact with the Central Asian mounted nomads, and in due course transmitted these stimuli, such as the animal style in art, to Indonesia and Oceania. The extent of the influence of Asian centres on America is hard to gauge, but in Mexico and Peru the essentials of mature culture were developed in urban form, in the midst of agriculturalist and hunter peoples, who in some cases pursued their more primitive existence until the time of the Spanish conquest (1520–1530 AD).

EUROPE'S LAST PRIMITIVE CULTURES

The influence of the city-civilisations of western Asia on Europe's primitive cultures in the Neolithic era and the Bronze Age is apparent in archaeological finds through the whole of this period. The art of Europe was a response to the stimulus—indeed, to the challenge—of the advanced urban cultures of the eastern Mediterranean lands. Agriculture had come from the Middle East, and now pottery and its ornamental repertory followed from the same source. We have here the first example in history—it could not have happened until the rise of the first mature cultures —of that interaction between high and primitive cultures which has continued until modern times.

Neolithic cultures appeared in the Aegean, the Balkans and southern Europe from about 4000 BC and spread to western and northern Europe from about 2500 BC. Bronze-using cultures followed in the same regions around 3000 and 2000 BC respectively. These influences were spread by two great natural routes. One was the Danube basin, leading to Central Europe, the other was the sea coasts of the Mediterranean and the Atlantic, leading to the north.

Cultural traffic was already in progress in the Neolithic period.

From about 3000 BC until after 1000 BC graves in south-eastern Europe contained small female figurines in clay of the 'Great Mother' type, a symbol of oriental fertility beliefs. These portable Neolithic idols were often extremely simple and no more than a cipher, a small, flat clay tablet with an emblem scratched on it. Only in the Bronze Age (second millennium BC) did the figurines take on distinct and recognisably human features, perhaps under influences from Minoan Crete. The 'Cycladic' idols, which appeal so strongly to twentieth-century eyes, were a development in marble of the clay figurines.

The first wave of decorated pottery vessels to reach Europe was ribbon-decorated ware *(Bandkeramik)* and it gives us a means of tracing the progress of the spiral motif as it gradually spread from its source in western Asia, up the Danube, into Central Europe. The ribbons were painted on the surface as far as the neighbourhood of Prague. Farther west, they were incised. The climax of the spiral ornamentation on pottery occurred in what is known as phase 2 of the northern European Bronze Age (about 1400–1200 BC). The spirals subsequently turned into undulating lines in phases 3 (about 1200–1000 BC) and 4 (about 1000–900 BC). Finally a style of free decoration with animal motifs prevailed in phase 5 (about 900–750 BC).

The sea route round the coasts, on the other hand, served to spread the megalithic ('big-stone') culture with its characteristic monumental stone structures. The megalithic people were clearly farmers and we can even recognise the cereals which they planted. They had cows, pigs and goats as domestic animals and, towards the end of

the period, horses as well. They had a well-developed cult of the dead and their ambitious sanctuaries and tomb-mounds are scattered through southern and western Europe. The inspiration for these came through contact with the mature cultures of the Middle East, principally Egypt (as is borne out by green turquoise beads of almost certainly Egyptian origin, found in megalithic tombs in Spain and Brittany). It was taken up by the Cretans (the palace at Knossos was built about 2000 BC and destroyed about 1400 BC) and spread *via* Malta (second millennium BC) to Spain, France, Ireland and northern Europe. The standing stones of western France are dated between 2000 and 1800 BC and the megalithic graves between 1800 and 1400 BC.

The crowning achievement of megalithic architecture is Stonehenge on Salisbury Plain in southern England. The enigma of the purpose of this majestic structure of upright stones between 12 and 22 feet in height has long puzzled archaeologists, but it now seems almost certain that it was not only a temple, but that the alignments were planned so as to make it function as a sophisticated astronomical observatory. Stonehenge was built in several phases, roughly between 1900 and 1600 BC. Contacts with Egypt would explain how the necessary astronomical knowledge was acquired.

The spiral as a motif in stone carving came by the same maritime route. It appeared as a relief on upright slabs in the temple at Hal Tarxien in Malta (second millennium) and was frequently incised on the walls of passage graves in Brittany and Ireland (for example, at New Grange). Spirals also occur in the Scandinavian and German rock pictures of about 1000 BC, though the ship motif predominated. An important group of Bronze Age rock pictures was engraved on boulders in the Val Camonica in the Italian Alps which includes chariots and bull's heads. The chariot was at this time growing in importance as an object of worship, and the sun-chariot from Trundholm in Denmark (between 1400 and 1200 BC) and the famous bronze chariot from Strettweg in Styria (about 700 BC) were fashioned for religious use. These examples of representational metal-work, to which standing human figures were often added, were forerunners of the archaic bronze sculpture which flourished around 500 BC. The 'nuraghic' bronze figurines from Sardinia are the finest examples.

Europe's last important primitive cultures flourished during the second half of the first millennium BC. They were the Iron Age Hallstatt culture in Austria and, from the fourth century BC onward, the La Tène culture among Celtic peoples in western Europe. Hallstatt art, and especially La Tène art, was highly accomplished and had affinities with the style of the nomads in the steppes of Russia and Central Asia which will be discussed in the following section. Even more distant affinities present themselves with the early art of the South-East Asian Bronze Age, a phenomenon of great interest which will be discussed in the chapter on Indonesia.

28 (above). **Engraved back of a British bronze mirror** from Desborough, Northamptonshire. 1st century AD. $10\frac{5}{8}$ in. (27 cm.). British Museum, London.
29 (below). **Inlaid bronze wine ewer** from Basse-Yutz (Moselle) (detail). Early La Tène culture. h. (of whole ewer) $15\frac{1}{2}$ in. (39.4 cm.). British Museum, London. The Celtic peoples brought the primitive art of Europe to its apogee and developed a style that survived the high culture of the Roman Empire, to reappear in the early Middle Ages. The decoration of the handle and spout (below) uses mounted nomad motifs. The sophisticated spiral design (above) has links with both S.-E. Asian and Celtic Christian art.

The Nomads

At some time from the third millennium onward, the people inhabiting the great steppes that extend almost without natural obstacles across eastern Europe and western Asia from the Carpathians to the Pamirs turned from primitive food-gathering to cattle herding. Then, with the taming of the horse as a means of transport, coupled with the use of the chariot, this pastoral way of life developed, for some of them, into mounted nomadism. The chariot itself, a lumbering affair drawn by asses, had been invented by the Sumerians about 3000 BC, but the wild horse was not native to the Middle East, and the development of the chariot as a swift and deadly weapon had to await the introduction of horses by invaders from the north.

The first record of mounted warriors is in a carved relief of the fifteenth or fourteenth century BC, from Tell Halaf in northern Syria, where the local Hurrians were subject to invading Indo-European overlords from beyond the Caucasus. The horse-drawn chariot was the basis of the military power of the agressive Hittites who, also coming from the north, entrenched themselves in Anatolia about 2000 BC. The steppes were ideally suited to the movements both of horse and waggon, and once the new nomadic peoples were equipped in this way, they were able to spread out over the entire extent of the steppes, so that their presence was felt in equal measure in Europe, in the Middle East and in China.

The art of the nomadic peoples was rooted in the beliefs of shamanism, which have already been described. Motifs derived from the shamanism of the early hunter period had, in some cases, acquired a later form at the hands of the mature cultures of western Asia, and these sophisticated re-statements of ancient motifs were re-introduced to the nomads, who, being closer to an earlier stage of human development, recognised their original content and readily adopted them.

Theirs was a decorative art in wood, metal and leather, for use on saddlery, tents and movable goods. Knotted rugs were probably made at an early date, although the famous rug found in a frozen tomb at Pazyryk in the Altai mountains of Siberia may have been an importation from Central Asia. It is nevertheless significant in showing naturalistic stags and horsemen in the borders. The alteration in the way of life of those of the steppe peoples who, as a result of various influences, turned nomad during the first millennium BC, was reflected in a marked change of vision on the part of their artists. With the loss of the hunter culture in its pure state went a gradual retreat from naturalism and an

15, 16

CHART E: THE HORSE IN ANCIENT TIMES AND THE CULTURES OF THE STEPPES

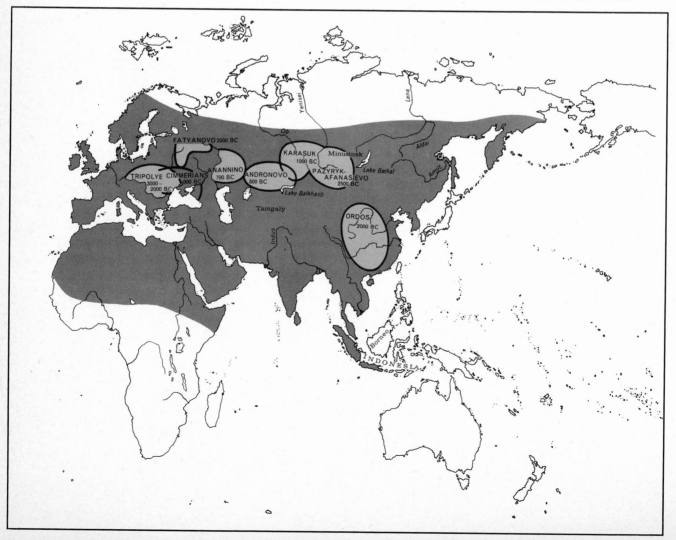

increasing stylisation of motifs which had originally been based on constant observation of familiar wild life. The hunting-magical purpose that underlay the ancient naturalistic animal style was probably understood longer by the nomads, due to the beliefs of shamanism which they long continued to profess.

In due course the nomads handed the motifs on to other peoples with whom they came into contact. In this way, nomadic art had an influence on Central Asia, China and even, through China, on Indonesia. It had a late influence on western European art, too, during the upheavals of the fifth and sixth centuries AD, when the barbarian peoples overran the Roman world under pressures from the east. The nomads continued the animal-style art of the hunter peoples, the principal motifs of which now were, (A) the animal glancing backwards, (B) the beast of prey at the throat of its victim, (C) the open-work style which may have been derived from the prehistoric X-ray style, and (D) the stag. The specific contributions to this repertoire by the nomadic artists were the animal's body constructed out of various dismembered parts, and the decoration of the animal's body with spirals, the origin of which is discussed below. During the first millennium BC all of these motifs were spread outward from Central Asia into China and so to the areas bordering the south-east of China, where they are finally lost in abstractions, the origin of which can scarcely be identified even by the trained eye.

THE X-RAY STYLE, THE SPIRAL AND THE STAG

The X-ray style occurs not only in the prehistoric rock pictures made by the early hunters in Scandinavia and Siberia. It has continued in use as late as this century in the ornamental art of native Siberian hunters like the Ostiaks, and in America among the Eskimos and Indians of the North-West, fading away at last among the Pueblo Indians of the South-West. The magic rites which are practised by the Ojibwa (Chippewa) people of the northern U.S.A. and Canada include the drawing of images in the X-ray style, and can still be observed. Rock pictures in the X-ray style occur in Kansas, Minnesota and Virginia, though they are difficult to make out. The final offshoots reach Panama (gold ornaments) and the Waika tribe in Venezuela (modern drawings). It is a curious fact that on all continents the X-ray style stops short of the full extension of the early hunters' original animal style. In America, it is not found south of the equator; in Australia, not south of Arnhem Land; and in Africa not at all.

The same tendency towards abstraction that we have

30. Siberian rock picture of a hind looking backward. Copy of a punched-out engraving from the upper Yenisei river, Shalabolinsk district. l. 9 in. (23 cm.). From a plaster cast in the Archaeological collection of the Academy of Sciences, Leningrad. Rock pictures from this region (Minusinsk) show the X-ray style in transition. Abstractions (vertical stripes, scrolls) ended up as the open-work style of the mounted nomads.

31. Abstraction of the X-ray style. (*a*) Copy of an Eskimo drawing of a seal from Alaska. (*b*) Copy of a rock painting of a fish from McCluer gulf, western New Guinea. (*c, d, e*) Copies of modern aboriginal bark paintings of fish from Arnhem Land. The spine and inner organs, at first fairly realistic, turn into criss-cross lines and finally the outline itself dissolves in an abstract pattern.

already noticed in the Siberian rock pictures can be followed in X-ray images found in India, Malaya, western New Guinea and in Arnhem Land, but without the trend toward either spiral ornament or the open-work style. Instead, the trend is to dissolve the design in lozenges—particularly noticeable in the bark paintings of the Australian Northern Territory. The earliest bark paintings, found in Field Island in 1884, featured a pure X-ray style. A tendency toward stylisation appeared in the bark paintings from Goulburn Island made in the nineteen-thirties, and more so in recent years. In pictures of kangaroos or fish, for example, one can clearly see the internal organs shown with a certain anatomical fidelity at one stage, then gradually superseded by hatched lozenges, until finally the whole figure was absorbed in abstractions.

This development, observed at work over the last eighty years, and the fact that the X-ray style in the rock and bark paintings of Arnhem Land is confined to a closely circumscribed area, suggest that it derives from an external stimulus which affected only the northern coast of Australia and may even be fairly recent. The Marind-anim in southern New Guinea, have kept an X-ray style tradition alive to the present day, and a similar tradition is evident in the old rock pictures of western New Guinea, so a glance at the map shows rock pictures executed in X-ray style occurring all the way from Norway, *via* northern Asia, to South America and appearing in a second area extending from India, *via* the Malayan peninsula, to western New Guinea and northern Australia.

The tendency toward abstraction can be traced back to the nomad artists of Central Asia, and it is exemplified by their own treatment of the X-ray style, which they were using from the beginning of the second millennium BC. As the meaning of the inner lines, representing the heart and other vital organs, receded in importance with the changed way of life, so the lines became gradually more abstract. The naturalistic drawing of the pure hunter style evolved into a surface decoration with spirals. The intestines turned into coils or concentric circles, the artist's vision altering at a moment when the spiral as such had been introduced as a decorative motif into south Russia with the Tripolye culture about 2500 BC. The spiral was adopted by the nomads and was employed in the rock pictures on the upper Yenisei river in Siberia. The looser spiral forms of the mature cultures to the southward were also adopted later on and superimposed as modelled reliefs on the animal bronzes of the Ordos type.

The ornamentation often takes grotesque forms in the late animal style of the nomads. The bodies seem to have been dismembered and put together again with unrelated heads, wings, claws and other parts. This style appears in China in the Shang period (about 1500–1000 BC) and reaches its fullest development under the Chou dynasty (about 1000–255 BC). Before supplanting the Shang rulers, the Chou had had close connections with the Central Asian nomads on the north-western borders of the empire. The

32. **Chinese horse of the late Chou period.** Copy of the design on a tile. (After Eleanor Consten *Das Alte China*, Stuttgart, 1958.) The interior lines derive from vestiges of the X-ray style in mounted nomad art, which influenced China during the 1st millennium BC. A formal surface ornamentation of spirals developed from this and spread to S.-E. Asia and Oceania.

33. **A wallaby from New Guinea.** Copy of a modern painting by the Marind-Anim. (After Paul Wirz *Die Marind-Anim*, Hamburg, 1922.) An example of the pure X-ray style in use.

34. **Copy of a modern Aboriginal bark painting of a kangaroo** from Goulburn island, Arnhem Land. Original in the National Museum of Victoria, Melbourne. The X-ray style is still obvious, but an abstract pattern is encroaching.

remains of a squatting figure carved in stone, decorated with free spirals, have been found in the excavations of the great Shang period capital at Hsiao T'un near Anyang in north Honan, dated between 2000 and 1250 BC. The *38* spirals may have been intended to suggest body painting. In this figure, two important south-east Asian motifs—the squatting figure and the spiral—are already combined at a very early date.

In Oceania as a whole, the spiral seems to have accompanied the spread of the south-east Asian Dongson culture (see page 77), around 300 BC. The spirals of New *36* Zealand, and especially the spiral derivatives in the *51* Marquesas islands, point to an association with the spirals of the late Chou period in China. In his recent work on the settlement of the Marquesas, H. L. Shapiro gives a firm date of 200 BC for this event, so that from a chronological point of view, a connection is at least plausible. The further diffusion of the spiral motif in America is described on pages 135–6.

One of the very ancient motifs revived or developed by the nomads was the stag. Representations of these favourite animals of the chase were included in the cave paintings of the Magdalenian period and later in the Spanish Levant style. The latter's affinities with frescoes at Çatal Hüyük in Anatolia (already mentioned on page 48) lead us to look to that quarter, where we find representations of stags dating from about the same period. Throughout the second and first millennia BC the stag was the most frequently portrayed animal in an area extending from eastern Spain to the *14* Ordos Steppe in north-western China. Stags—all treated with a similar feeling for scale—occur at various times during the first six thousand years BC, in the Nuraghic bronzes of Sardinia, in Scythian metalwork, in bronzes from Minusinsk in eastern Siberia and in the Tamgaly rock pictures. The nomads can be supposed to have been the *27* agents in disseminating this motif, especially as they are known to have been fond of ordering stag figurines from artists in the Greek colonies on the coast of the Black Sea and in the Ordos Steppe.

Representations of stags did not spread to Africa, but scenes of men in action, whose origin is related to that of the animals-and-humans pictures of the Spanish Levant style, go right through Africa from north to south. These were as lively in Bushman art as they were in eastern Spain, and give us yet another example of how the early hunter style lent itself to adaptation and of how variously the early mature cultures influenced the primitive hunters of all periods. In the chapter on Indonesia, this process will be clearly traced from historical evidence.

THE HERDSMEN AND FARMERS OF THE ASIAN STEPPES

Between the third and the first millennium BC, several *E* cultures of farmers and herdsmen developed in the Eurasian Steppe. The most important were, firstly, the 'Tripolye' culture in south Russia, between 3000 and 1700 BC; secondly, the 'Afanasievo' culture in the Minusinsk basin

of eastern Siberia, also between 3000 and 1700 BC; thirdly, its sequel in the Minusinsk basin, the 'Karasuk' culture, about 1000 BC. Each of these cultures was the recipient of motifs from nomadic art and they also diffused such motifs as the spiral, which come from the ornamental repertoire of the mature cultures. Through the pastoral cultures and the nomads these motifs spread eastwards to China and thence were exported to Oceania and America.

The 'Tripolye' culture made extensive use of the spiral as an ornament, and it is a reasonable guess that spiral ornamentation spread from the Ukraine both westwards up the Danube and eastwards to China, where it left its mark on Kansu ceramic ware (2000–1200 BC), and on **30** Jōmon pottery in Japan (about 1000 BC). By about the time *35* of Christ it had reached western Alaska, the site of the 'Old Bering Sea' culture. (The Old Bering Sea culture is known from archaeological finds only, and is the basis of Eskimo culture. One feature of the finds consists of carved walrus-ivory leg-chains for which there must have been iron prototypes, now lost. The probable dates are 100 BC–400 AD.)

THE NOMAD STYLE IN CHINA AND SOUTH-EAST ASIA

How the nomad style spread beyond the borders of China cannot be understood without first knowing something about the nature of Chinese art itself, down to the Han period (roughly 200 BC to 200 AD). This will, incidentally, provide an impressive example of animal motifs from the world of northern Asia's primitive hunters being transmitted by the mounted nomads to the mature cultures of the Middle East, returning as reformulated decorative motifs in the minor arts and being carried, again by the mounted nomads, to the borders of China, where they are adopted, naturalised and modified, and passed on in the course of Chinese cultural expansion, to the innermost parts of Indonesia and Oceania.

The early development of Chinese art can be read in the magnificent bronze vessels of the Shang and Chou periods. **21** They first appear about 1500 BC with a fully-fledged abstract ornamental style adapted from Shang ceramic ware. Before long, this gives way to animal designs. The bronzes are very often decorated with a characteristic 'monster mask' motif *(t'ao t'ieh)* which is hard to connect with any natural model but may be derived from the full-face snarling tiger. (Apart from their frequent occurrence **20** in Chinese art, tiger-motifs are also found in the western fringes of the Pacific Ocean, for example in Borneo, where they are derived from the popular Chinese savage-animal masks; in America the same tiger motif appears in the native form of the ocelot or jaguar). Other animals which can be identified on Shang bronzes include elephants, fish and, not least, the dragon. Exactly what natural prototype the dragon was based on is unknown, and it did not in fact acquire a definitive form until the Han era, as will be discussed below. The earlier dragons were very varied, but there are written descriptions which help us to identify

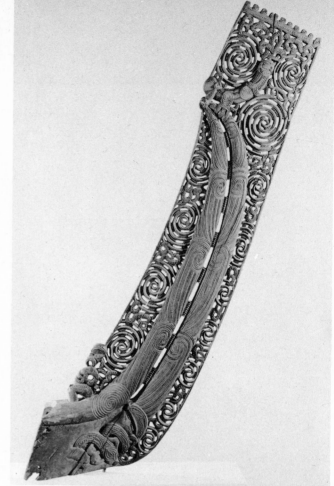

35 (above). **Neolithic Japanse vase** from Harino-uchi shellmound, Ichikawa City, Chiba-ken. Late Jōmon period, 1st millennium BC. Baked and incised clay. h. 1 ft. 8 in. (50.7 cm.). National Museum, Tokyo.

36 (right). **Maori canoe prow ornament** from New Zealand Carved Wood h. 4 ft. 11 in. (150 cm.). Museum für Völkerkunde, Munich. Spiral patterns of this fluent, decorative type were carried from the mainland of Asia to prehistoric Japan, and across the ocean by the seafaring Polynesians to New Zealand, where it proliferates in all Maori art.

37 (below). **Stone tjuringa from Central Australia.** 19th–20th century. The most sacred objects in the lives of the Aborigines, *tjuringas* (or *churingas*) are often carved with spirals, of great symbolic importance to their owners. The wholly abstract forms have an affinity with 20th-century western art.

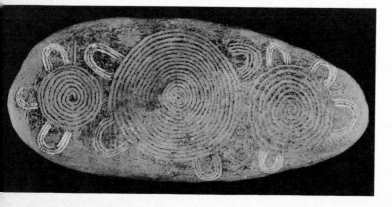

them in their often unfamiliar forms. Mountain and forest dragons are mentioned in the *Book of Songs (Shih-Ching)*, living in trees and having only one leg. They are said to be the ancestors of the people and princes of the central Chinese provinces of Honan, Hopei and Hunan. These one-legged dragons are often found on the ritual bronzes of the Chou period.

The Chou animal style lasted about five hundred years and ended in the ninth or eighth century BC. In the seventh century a new and different style began to spread through China: the so-called Huai style, previously also known as the Ch'in style on the assumption that it lasted only for a short period during the Ch'in Dynasty (249–202 BC). It has now been assigned by scholars to far earlier dates, and this style takes its name from finds in the Huai Valley, dating from the sixth century.

The Huai style is clearly distinguishable from the one that went before. Characteristic are the figures of tigers with heads lowered, usually affixed as handles to bells and vessels. They exhibit a distinct relationship with Central Asian animal figures. Very striking are the S-shaped dragons and dragons bent at a right angle, which are frequently intertwined and in many instances reduced to pure linear ornament. These renderings are closely related to the plaited band, which likewise occurs frequently. Both point to foreign influences, as does the granulation which now comes into frequent use—a technique whereby the surface is incrusted with a close pattern of tiny raised dots of metal.

38. **Drawing of a Neolithic Chinese carved stone squatting figure from Anyang.** *c.* 2000–1050 BC. Excavated at Hsiao-t'un, Anyang (on the site of the Shang dynasty capital) and illustrated in *Archaeology in China* by Cheng Tê-k'un, 1960, Vol. II, p. 107. Weighing 34 lbs (15.4 kg.), this marble figure was a carved ornament fixed to a building by lime plaster, remains of which still adhere to its back. It is roughly contemporary with the Pan Shan ware in plate 30, or only a little later, and the loose, open spirals are the earliest evidence we have of the use of this motif in Chinese art other than on pottery. It is significant to find the spiral and squatting figure motifs combined so early in the history of eastern Asia.

There are good reasons for assuming that expansion did not halt there, but pressed on as far as Indonesia. The advance towards the north was resumed during the Han Dynasty (202 BC–226 AD). Warfare against the mounted peoples from Central Asia was persistent and hard. To resist the highly trained bodies of heavy and light cavalry, the Chinese had to make radical changes in their armament and in their whole military system, and it is likely that 'sinicised' nomad tribes played an essential part in this reorganisation. Finds in Han graves contain quantities of weapons and armour of a new type: chain-mail, long swords, standards, stirrups, a new type of bridle, and belts with metal plates and a particular type of clasp. The Chinese took these items of equipment over directly from the Sarmatians, who dominated the central steppes during early Han times, although they probably originated with the Saka peoples.

It was the decorated belt-clasps which exerted the greatest influence on Chinese art. In keeping with the custom of the mounted nomads, they are covered with animal figures, strictly stylised, yet with tremendous vitality. The pottery found in Han graves, especially the models of horses, has its roots in this style. Most of the belt-clasps represent animals locked in combat. The animal style already being familiar in China, these scenes had great appeal there and were repeated in large quantities until they had gradually become imbued with Chinese feeling. Numerous figures show each of the intermediate stages in the process of transformation: the barbaric mobility of the figures slowly cedes to softness and elegance of line, and from this fusion there finally results an incomparable harmonious composition.

The development from Huai to Han style gave the dragon its definitive form. It emerges, the synthesis of various traditions, as the supple and lively creature we know. The enigmatic creatures of the Chou period disappear and later modifications will only be minor. It is a quadruped with an elongated, scaly body and a horned head, its jaw open and both lips rolled back to reveal its fangs; the feet are like an eagle's talons. (The intertwined snakes of the Huai can confidently be classed as dragons too, since in China, snakes are regarded as just one of the dragon's manifestations).

Chinese history books also support an early dating of the Huai style and at the same time explain the strong foreign influence. In the great history called *Shih-Chi*, written in the Han period, we are told that in the seventh century BC, the Tik and Dzong (or Jung) tribes from northern Asia invaded China and penetrated as far as Honan, when they were subjugated by the energetic princes of the state of Ch'in and settled locally, mainly in the Huai Valley in the south of Honan province. Thus we have evidence at this early date for nomads from central Asia making deep inroads into China. According to the dating by Professor De Groot of an account in the penultimate book of the *Book of Songs* this invasion was preceded during the tenth or eleventh century BC by another, that of the I tribe, who were defeated on the banks of the River Huai by the armies of the state of Lu. Although the cultural influence of the first recorded nomadic invasion is uncertain, the second clearly gave Chinese art a new direction. During the next period there was no end to these nomadic inroads.

When the Ch'in put an end to the Chou Dynasty in 249 BC, they were regarded by the Chinese as semi-barbarians, since they had intermarried extensively with nomads in their north-western homeland. Under Ch'in rule the empire was consolidated. In the north, the Great Wall was strengthened and extended to keep the barbarians out, and there was extensive settlement towards the south, reaching the coast in the area of modern Hong Kong.

Indonesia and Oceania

SOUTH-EAST ASIA IN PREHISTORY

In the late Pleistocene, over 250,000 years ago, when the northern hemisphere was locked in its most protracted Ice Age, Indonesia in the widest sense, including Malaya and the Philippines, constituted a land bridge between Asia and Australia. It was then that the hominid known as *Pithecanthropus* ('Peking Man', 'Java Man', 'Heidelberg Man') made his way south to Java. He did not live in Australia, which appears to have been first reached at a later epoch by migrant peoples with some sort of craft after the melting of the great ice caps had raised the level of the ocean and created the island chains we know today. These were groups of hunters and food gatherers who traversed the whole of Indonesia and Australia. Their surviving representatives are still found in remote districts of New Guinea, the Philippines and Malaya, no longer typical of the racial or cultural composition of the region as a whole. From the first millennium BC, Indonesia has been the domain of food-producing peoples—one group Neolithic, the other group of Bronze and Iron Age culture—who spread out over the islands from South-East Asia.

The two groups, which co-existed in many areas, need to be distinguished from one another. The earlier of them, which had the more lasting effects, were the ancient Austronesians who reached the islands from their homeland in south China about 1500 BC. At this period, the whole area became the centre of Neolithic farmer cultures which eventually expanded across the Pacific and Indian Oceans. Such long sea-borne expeditions presuppose boat-building of a fairly advanced kind; the Polynesians, whose culture was wholly Neolithic when the Europeans explored the Pacific in the eighteenth century, made ocean voyages over several thousand miles, with hundreds of people and domestic animals aboard huge carvel-built canoes.

Typical of this culture throughout South-East Asia are two implements known to archaeologists from their shape and section as the 'quadrangular adze' and the 'round axe' respectively. Examples of the latter are found in Melanesia and East Africa as well. The monuments are megalithic: menhirs, dolmens, stone 'spirit-seats' and platforms, pyramids, stone-girdled mounds, fortifications, stairways, paved paths and meeting places. In Sumatra the remains

33

CHART F: SOUTH-EAST ASIA, INDONESIA, MELANESIA AND NORTHERN AUSTRALIA

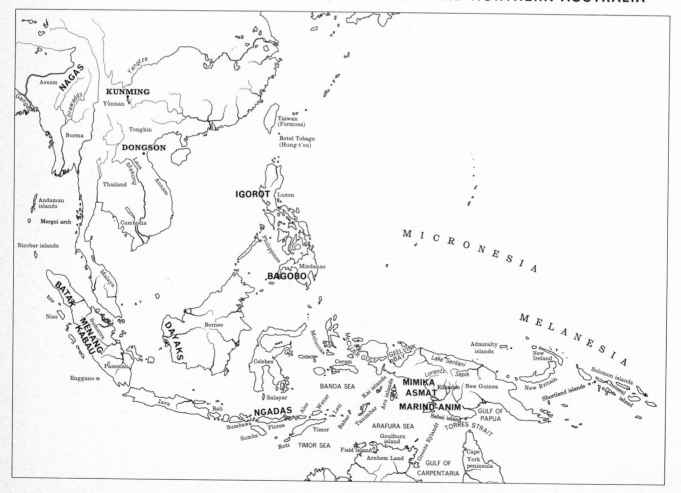

are widespread, and continue to modern times. The most important examples are on the Pasemah plateau in southern Sumatra where there are large numbers of free-standing carved figures of men and animals.

The way in which the statues that stand in the Pasemah grave fields were made strongly suggests that they were a development of the megalithic tradition of erecting large standing stones. The Pasemah artists seem to have taken the natural form of the block as their starting point, as if they had first read a figure or scene into the shape and only then tried to make sculptural use of its possibilities. The figures appear to be conceived in the round, but on looking at them more closely, one often discovers that they are really a combination of profile and frontal views in relief, in a technique that is reminiscent of Chinese tomb carvings of the Han period. It is interesting to compare the stone ox at Geramat in Sumatra with a carved block found in the tomb at Hsing-p'ing (Shensi) of a Chinese general, Huo k'iu-ping, who had died in 117 BC. This block had been modelled to give the impression of a group in the round by two-dimensional relief carving on all sides, without greatly changing the natural form of the stone. The Han group shows a demon trying to devour an animal, in a manner very like the Pasemah scenes of fighting animals.

Many Pasemah carvings represent bronze swords, rings and, especially, drums by which the sculpture can be dated and its place assessed in the Bronze and Iron Age culture that spread through South-East Asia. The possibility of Indian influence showing in the movement of the carved figures is, however, still an open question.

A megalithic culture is still flourishing today among the Nagas of Assam, and survives in the mountains of Vietnam and in Luzon in the Philippines. Its vigour and adaptability have been astonishing. When the Khasi and Jaintia peoples of Assam, whose culture was at the megalithic stage, were confronted with Indian civilisation about 1500 AD their own culture, instead of being eliminated by the mature one, was actually diffused as a result over a still wider area and new artistic themes enriched their repertoire. Their own way of life continued unshaken. Likewise, contact with India under British rule led the Agami to make practical improvements in their megalithic architecture.

A good place to see how many variations are capable of developing in megalithic culture is on the island of Nias, off the west coast of Sumatra, where there is a profusion of local styles with a rich exuberance of forms.

The age of metal in South-East Asia, with the almost simultaneous appearance of bronze and iron, began between 150 BC and 50 AD. The principal Bronze Age culture takes the name of 'Dongson' from a village in north Vietnam where burials were systematically excavated and dated to the middle of the first century AD by the discovery of Chinese Han dynasty objects and of some coins minted in the reign of the Emperor Wang Mang (9–23 AD). The site has provided the type-implement for this culture, a well-made socketed bronze axe which suggests an origin in

39. **Carved wooden door panel from Taiwan** (Formosa), inlaid with mother-of-pearl. h. 5 ft. 7 in. (170 cm.). Ethnographical collection of Zürich University. This modern carving by the non-Chinese natives combines rifles and bandoliers with distinct motifs of the S.-E. Asian Neolithic farmer cultures. We see the 'snake of heaven' descending over the man's head and in the form of an arched snake with a head at both ends (see plates 76, 77); the spiral motif in the coiled snake round the keyhole; the skull-cult motif in the two heads above; and, above all, the 'bent-knees' ancestor figure of Polynesian type in the centre.

China and thus, through Siberia, ultimately in the European bronze age. Population pressure in China at about the time of Christ, and probably much earlier, seems to have set off a series of extensive immigrations by peoples in south China and South-East Asia generally. The direction was always southwards across the islands, and similar movements have continued right through history, as the consequence of a wasteful scorched-earth agriculture. Traces of metal working are found all the way to eastern Indonesia, the most distant find so far being a bronze axe head from Lake Sentani in northern New Guinea.

The conditions in which the Dongson people lived may be seen, in all probability, in the life of the peoples who inherited their culture and kept it almost unchanged from that time to this. These are, for example, the Dayaks of Borneo and the Bataks and others in Sumatra. The Dongson culture was supported by a primitive feudal society presided over by a chieftain and centred on the communal club-houses that are still a feature of life in many South-East Asian and Oceanic communities. Family groups will have been large and the fields will have been tilled in com-

mon. There is evidence of a strongly developed ancestor cult with a megalithic accent. There was much business of placing large stones and carved ancestor figures and of constructing monumental tombs. Apart from these carvings in stone, bronze was the characteristic artistic medium and great bronze drums were the characteristic form. The ornamental-fanciful style which still flourishes in Borneo had already appeared. The decoration of the drum gives us a great deal of our information about the Dongson culture. Some of the ornamentation is abstracted beyond recognition, but it is possible to make out scenes of funeral dancers and of other ritual or communal activities.

44, 45, 4[

Recent excavations at a site in south-western China (Shih-chai-shan near Kunming, Yünnan) have brought to light a quantity of bronze objects which help us to locate the sources of the Dongson culture. The Shih-chai-shan culture seems to have existed independently of the encroaching Chinese culture and, while adopting some elements of Chinese art, to have drawn its style mainly from western sources. Its affinities are more with the Bronze Age in Siberia and Europe. Pictures on bronze drums tell

28, 29, 4[

CHART G: THE DIFFUSION OF THE SPIRAL MOTIF

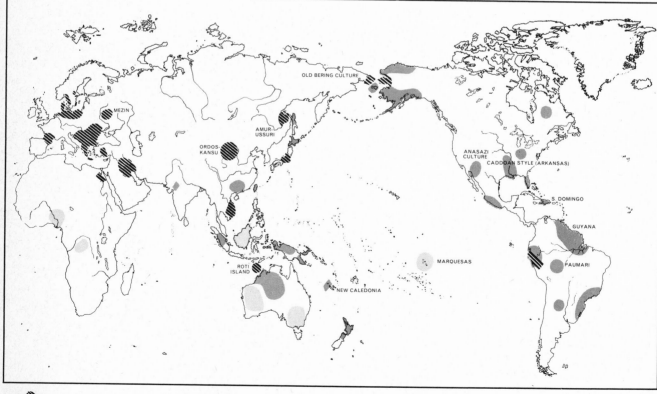

 Area of the distinct spiral motif   Areas where derivatives of the spiral occur   Attenuated spiral motifs

41. **Painting from Gaua Island,** Banks group, New Hebrides, Melanesia. 19th century. Wood. h. 27½ in. (70 cm.). Museum für Völkerkunde, Munich. Painted with the assurance that comes from a long tradition, this is a classic squatting figure as translated from sculpture to the plane. The stylised ribs, which have merged with the vertebrae all the way down the spine, indicate that the picture represents the spirit of a dead ancestor. The decorations are of a fanciful kind, probably borrowed from European models, and no longer refer to the native mythology. The panel is a board from a chest of European origin.

42. **Carved spoon from N. Luzon,**
Philippines. 19th century. Wood.
l. 8 in. (20 cm.). Museum für Völkerkunde, Munich. The importance and
prevalence of the squatting ancestor
figure is illustrated here by its use on a
household object. In spite of this, it keeps
its sacramental dignity. The problem of
relating the conical figure to the stem and
bowl has been solved without
awkwardness.

43. **Roof ornament from the Sepik River Valley,** New Guinea. 19th century. Fired clay. h. 19¼ in. (49 cm.). Museum für Völkerkunde, Munich. Sepik Valley art (see also plates 32, 67, 69, 73), with its exuberance and swirling, spiral-derived lines, developed a richness of form exceeding that of any other part of Oceania. The squatting figure here has been given a female identity and a fertility emphasis, connecting it with the Indian 'nude goddess' motif. A mythical bird stretches its protective wings overhead. The same hubbed discs decorate the Sepik face-urn in plate 73.

44 (opposite). **Painted shield from south-eastern Borneo.** Late 19th century. Wood. h. 27½ in. (70 cm.). Rijksmuseum voor Volkenkunde, Leiden. In Borneo, the influence of the Dongson culture (*c.* 300 BC) and of early Chinese art produced an 'ornamental-fanciful' style with a strong sense of linear decoration. The symmetrical composition on this shield—two squatting ancestor figures in an abstract copulation scene—was widely used to ward off evil.

45. **Veil in Nazca style from southern Peru.** 400–600 AD. Woven llama wool. h. 3 ft. 7¼ in. (110 cm.). Museum für Völkerkunde, Munich. The same monumentality and bold colour is noticeable here as in the later Peruvian textile in plate 40. The highly formal, countercharged squatting figures may be emblems of day and night, or of some similar dual principles.

46 (opposite). **The god Xochipilli ('Flower Prince').** 15th century. Aztec culture, Mexico. Volcanic stone. h. 29½ in. (75 cm.). Museum für Völkerkunde, Mannheim.

47. **Squatting figure from Costa Rica.** Date unknown. Stone. h. 8 in. (20 cm.). Museum für Völkerkunde, Munich. Archaeologists have yet to discover precisely how Asia's influence reached America across the Pacific, but the existence of this influence in art can be seen for a fact in these two squatting figures from Central America. Plate 47 could easily be taken for a Melanesian figure, while the fine example of Aztec sculpture (plate 46) is an exact rendering of the wooden Babar Islands figures (plate 38). Plate 46 also shows the direct influence of the Chinese motif, derived from the early hunters, of a human protected by the spirit of an animal or bird (plate 21).

48 (opposite). **Uli figure from New Ireland, Melanesia.** Early 20th century Wood. h. 5 ft. 7 in. (170 cm.).

49. **Pair of figures from New Britain,** Melanesia. 19th century. Wood. h. 31½ in. (80 cm.). Both plates, Museum für Völkerkunde, Munich. Melanesian art is richly varied, lively and elaborate and much of it is intended to be seen in movement. The powerful bi-sexual statue is an *uli* or collective ancestor figure (note the offspring clustered round it). The oversized head, coxcomb headdress and plant fibre beard are typical for *uli* figures. The pair opposite are an ancestral couple. The colours used include some of European origin. All three figures exhibit the 'bent-knees' stance, an important variant of the squatting figure in Oceania and Africa.

50. **Red-figure bark painting from the Aird River delta,** Gulf of Papua, New Guinea. *c.* 1900. l. 31½ in. (80 cm.). British Museum, London. With very simple strokes, the Papuan artist evokes a shuffling, dusty line of feather-bedecked tribal dancers and the squatting circle of men with the elder. The noticeably Australian appearance of the dancers and the wallaby (perhaps an animal-ancestor spirit, as it is carrying a bag on its arm in the way Papuan men carry their small belongings around), suggest cultural contact with Australia. Motifs from New Guinea spread as far as Kimberley in the west and Victoria and New South Wales in the south-east. This painting also illustrates two stages of the squatting figure motif developing into a row of dancers.

51 (opposite). **Ancestor figure from the Admiralty Islands, Melanesia.** Early 20th century. Wood. h. 23¾ in. (60 cm.). Museum für Völkerkunde, Munich. This superb naturalistic sculpture in the Admiralty Islands style displays typical local features in the woman's close-cropped hair, the position of the open mouth and the ear-lobes enlarged by tribal custom. It is rare, however, for the figure to be glancing back over its shoulder. The decorations may represent body painting or tattooing. The very slight flexion of the legs is a reminder that this is an ancestor figure.

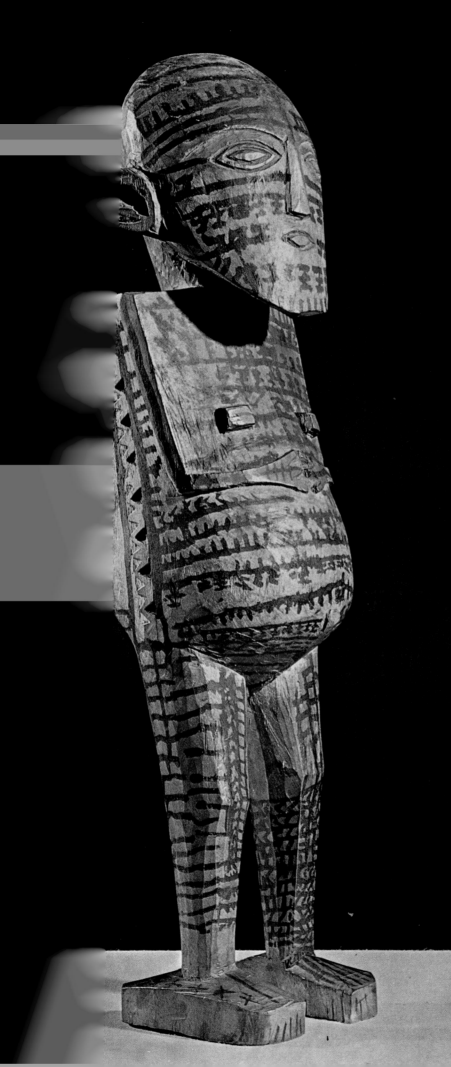

52. **Ancestor figure from the Cook Islands, Polynesia.** Probably early 18th century. Wood. h. 20 in. (50 cm.). Museum für Völkerkunde, Munich. Polynesian sculpture in the remote Cook Islands, between Tonga and Tahiti, tends to become monumental and abstract. Ornamental considerations alone seem to have guided the making of this rather passive, potbellied ancestor figure. Flexion of the legs is only vaguely indicated above the hammer-shaped feet.

53 (opposite). **Ancestor figure from Easter Island,** Polynesia. 19th century. Painted and stuffed bark cloth. h. 15½ in. (39.5 cm.). Peabody Museum, Harvard University. This fearsome doll, stuffed with bulrushes, was placed outside houses to ward off evil. The effects of the Easter Islanders' isolation show in the grotesque invention of the face, which also recalls the decorative style of Hawaii and the Maoris. In spite of possible influences from South America, Easter Island art is basically Polynesian (see plate 68).

54 (opposite). **Decorated bark cloth from Samoa,** Polynesia (detail). Early 20th century. h. (of whole piece) 6 ft. 10¼ in. (209 cm.). Museum für Völkerkunde, Munich. The black and yellow petals in the design could have developed from the pattern of concave 'arches' which are themselves an abstract version of squatting figures (see the chapter *Motif and Variation*).

55 (right). **Bowl of the Chimú culture,** Peru. 12th–13th centuries. Gourd inlaid with mother-of-pearl. Diameter 6½ in. (16.2 cm.).

56 (below). **Large bowl from Chama,** eastern Peru. 6th century. Clay. Diameter 12½ in. (32 cm.). Both plates, Museum für Völkerkunde, Munich. In America, too, squatting figures were often reduced to two-dimensional designs. On the cleverly inlaid gourd they form a ring round a central figure based on the same motif, but already with a tendency to abstraction. Fully abstract versions were taken over by the hunters or primitive farmers of the upper Amazon, as in the subtle decoration of this hand-made bowl.

57. **Chimú-style fabric,** northern Peru.
13th–15th century. Llama wool. h. 5 ft.
1¾ in. (157 cm.). Museum für Völkerkunde, Munich. The three warriors, each
holding a spear and a shrunken head
trophy in their hands, are clearly in the
squatting or, at least, the bent-knees
posture (the latter also came to signify a
figure in movement). The custom of
capturing heads for their own sakes,
which is found in many pre-Columbian
cultures and still survives in some parts of
South America, stems from S.-E. Asia. The
early farmers believed that as the head
was the seat of man's spiritual powers,
taking and collecting the heads of others
must be a means of enriching one's own
spiritual reserves.

spreading through Indonesia on the evidence of the bronze drums previously mentioned. The plaited band occurs very often on them and is found on one of the earliest drums yet known (one from Salayar Island off Celebes), although modified and no longer in the completely stylised form. The plaited band may still be encountered today in all those areas where the ornamental fanciful style survives. The hypothesis that it might have been introduced by the Muslims from India is refuted by the fact that it was closely associated with all the other spiral and spiral meander motifs of the Dongson culture.

The plaited band is important in Batak and Menang-kabau art on Sumatra, which is still very close to Dongson. Of sporadic occurrence on Bali, it is among the most important motifs in Borneo. It reaches Celebes, Timor and the Kai Islands close to New Guinea. Here it generally disintegrates into a pattern of parallel wavy lines, but it does appear in a carefully elaborated version on the crescent-shaped lower part of a carved wooden figure found in the Sepik river district of New Guinea.

In the following two sections, where we shall try to unravel the complex of influences which produced certain specifically Indonesian motifs in sculpture and decorative art, we will be able to put the foregoing investigations to good use. The stages of the diffusion of the plaited band motif, which have been traced from its presumed origin in western Asia to its final dissolution in eastern Indonesia, provide clues to the movements of cultures and peoples which are not recorded by history.

THE *Naga* OF BORNEO

Borneo art ranks high compared with the art of the other Indonesian islands, having absorbed many kinds of influence and fused them into an organic and individual style. The models are clearly indicated by various types of figure, and we can see it particularly clearly in the formation of the Borneo *naga*, in which the vigorous animal figures of the mounted nomads played a large part. Some *naga* figures derived directly from animal style models, 43 while others were based on the Chinese dragon in its definitive form—which in turn, as we have seen, was a product of nomad influence on Chinese art of an earlier period.

It is very interesting that motifs in a nomadic style that seems to be as yet unmodified by Chinese influence were introduced to Borneo independently of Chinese motifs in Huai, Ch'in and Han styles. The finest comparable piece to one from Borneo may sometimes be found in a very distant area of the nomad style—for example, objects from the Scythian barrow-graves of the first millennium BC near the mouth of the River Kuban in South Russia. A carved 42 awl-handle from Borneo, consisting of an animal with its head bent back, has an uncanny resemblance to a bronze 41 plaque from the Scythian 'Tomb of the Seven Brothers' (seventh to sixth century BC). The explanation could be that the bearers of such motifs moved across China rela-

tively quickly (perhaps as raiders or traders) or that they reached the coast *via* some more westerly route that did not touch China proper. The evidence of the Shih-chai-shan culture in south-western China, mentioned above, shows that influences from Central Asia passed that way, on the periphery of Chinese culture. But it seems that by the time they reached Borneo, these forms and motifs had lost their symbolic content—at least, the meaning of the figures was no longer clear enough to survive and to prevail against other interpretations. The form alone was adopted and filled with a different content of native origin.

Even though the figures from Borneo often invite direct comparison with those in pure animal style, it seems that these influences must have reached Borneo by way of China after all, since there are so many features similar to those that are known to have resulted when nomadic art was modified by the influence of Chinese art. What seems certain is that if the nomadic motifs found their way to Borneo through China they did so rapidly, since the modification is relatively slight.

There is a number of animal figures from Borneo, affixed to Dayak houses or implements, which we will now compare with those in nomadic animal style. Naturally we shall draw our comparison with objects from the Ordos Steppe, since this area was geographically closest to Borneo and the source of the animal which the Chinese also adopted. The animals are usually called by the natives *aso*, or dog. As already noted, this term can change its meaning without the image being modified much. The rendering of the dog

43. **Copy of a carved wooden naga as a gable ornament from Sumbawa Island,** Indonesia. Original in the Städtisches Völkerkundemuseum, Frankfurt-am-Main. Proliferating floral or feathery decoration, which almost make this a 'scroll-*naga*' (see pages 99–100), is barely held in check by the needs of a freestanding roofpiece, exposed to the wind.

was originally based upon that of a tiger, but since people did not care to speak the name of an animal as terrible as the tiger, they preferred to call it a dog. This is most significant, for firstly, a number of mounted nomad animal figures which can be considered as prototypes for those in Borneo are representations of feline animals, probably tigers; and secondly, we repeatedly find that the name given to an animal figure depends much less upon its content than upon the feelings of the viewer or artist himself, who sees in it whatever suits him best. Several entirely distinct animals, coming within the orbit of ideas strongly dominated by a particular animal, may all come to be interpreted as renderings of that one animal. Thus in Borneo, the tiger is changed into a dog and then, in the area where the dragon *naga* concept prevails, it is referred to as a *naga*.

Among the Borneo figures which lend themselves particularly well to comparison with those of the mounted nomads are the crouching animal with head raised, the same with its head turned backwards, animal groups, intertwined animals and, lastly, the curled-up animal. Fine examples of the first of these types are carved in relief on the Dayak doors.

44, 45, 46

28 Comparing these pieces with a belt-clasp from China, which has the Chinese version of a nomad theme, we find that there is, generally speaking, the same body curvature, crouching position of the forelegs, raised hind quarters and wide-open jaws. The twisted horn is also present. The rea-

son for the spirals on the shoulder and pelvic area of the animal from Borneo emerges: they are vestiges of what were once wings. It is not possible to find as convincing a parallel for the animal with its head turned backwards, but this motif occurs extremely frequently in nomad art. It often appears on bronze horse-trappings from the Ordos Steppe.

Another wooden carving from Borneo represents several animals which are hard to identify, because parts of them are so highly stylised, but native artists explained the characteristic features of the various parts of the body and what they were supposed to represent to the Dutch scholar A. W. Nieuwenhuis. According to them, the large animal, which it is easy to make out, has the head of another animal attached to the back of its own. This other animal has its legs pointing upwards. The features by which it may be identified are the two rows of teeth on the back of the first one and a huge fang pointing downwards. The eye of the second animal can now be picked out, the horn passes below the head of the larger animal and terminates as a tusk in its jaw. The body of the second animal passes in front of the head of the first one, the hind quarters and hind leg can be clearly identified and the tail is incorporated into the spiral ornamentation along the side.

Probably this is a further development of the original scene of animals locked in combat, one of the most favoured motifs in nomad art. If a horse is being attacked, it is usually depicted with the body in a characteristically distorted position, its hind quarters twisted upwards. This produces

a posture like that of the second animal in the Borneo carving. The disintegration of the Borneo animal's body into separate ornamental parts, which the viewer has some difficulty in fitting together again, is also characteristic of a number of Central Asian scenes of animals in combat when exposed to Chinese influence.

The influence of Central Asian art seems to make itself felt in other animal motifs from Borneo, although the parallels may be less pronounced. The similarities mentioned suffice to show that, among the many elements which go to make up the relatively advanced art of the Dayaks, one at least derives, whether directly or through China, from the art of the mounted nomads.

'SCROLL-*Naga*' AND 'MOTHER-*Naga*'

Two curious motifs which are peculiar to Indonesian art (and confined almost entirely to the eastern islands) appear at first sight to have no connection with mounted nomad art. These are known as the 'scroll-*naga*' and the 'mother-*naga*'. The former is confined to the island of Alor, and consists of a serpent-like body out of which an abundance of leafy ornament seems to be sprouting. The latter, of which the only known example outside eastern Indonesia comes from Borneo, consists of a *naga*-like creature with other similar creatures stacked in tiers above it.

The first clue to the origin of the scroll-*naga* is a drum from Alor which has its handles formed by two *nagas* in the shape of an 'S', with their tails meeting in the middle and their heads at each extremity. A very similar figure occurs in a tattoo pattern from Borneo, where we also find two animals merged together by the tail and a head at either end. This is a very common motif in nomadic art. A snake with a head at either end is found among the Ordos bronzes, among other pieces at every stage of stylisation, and frequently in Chinese works that were influenced by nomadic art. It is also found in the Amur area of eastern Siberia and in Taiwan (Formosa).

This evidence points to the spread of motifs of the Central Asian animal style as far afield as Indonesia and America, while the influence of the Chinese Huai style upon the ornamentation of the Ngada tribe on Flores has already been mentioned, but since most of the Huai style motifs stem from nomadic art, and since we have seen that the types of animal style on Borneo were only slightly modified by Chinese influence, it follows that the presence together in Indonesia of the Huai style and of the Central Asian animal style should be seen simply as the effect of different waves of a single cultural movement. The only distinction between them is the degree of Chinese influence which they absorbed respectively *en route*.

The mother-*naga* occurs frequently on Alor and there are scattered examples on Borneo and Timor where the child-

43

47 (above). **Chinese openwork bronze plaque of three 'stacked' ponies or asses.** Probably Han period, *c.* 200 BC–200 AD. h. 1½ in. (4 cm.). Museum für Völkerkunde, Munich. The almost affectionate distortion of the animal forms comes, like the stacking motif itself, straight from the mounted nomad style (see plate 25).

48 (below). **Chinese openwork bronze plaque of four couched does looking backward.** Han period, *c.* 200 BC–200 AD. h. 1½ in. (4 cm.). Museum für Völkerkunde, Munich. Chinese sensibility is reflected more definitely in this composition, but the motif is typical of the mounted nomads.

49 (left). **Two carved horn spoons from Timor,** Indonesia. Date unknown. h. 8½ in., 13¾ in., (22 cm., 35 cm.). Museum für Völkerkunde, Munich. The style on Timor islands was vigorous and the motifs that the artists used (squatting figures, spirals, birds with necks crossed, 'stacked' birds etc.) were treated in a distinctive way.

50 (above). **Copy of a carved wooden 'scroll-naga' from Alor** island, Indonesia. Original in the Städtisches Völker-kundemuseum, Frankfurt-am-Main. The tendency to dissolve form in abstract decoration is exemplified by comparing this subject with figure 43.

naga on her back often takes on the form of a bird. In this the *naga* motif merges significantly with the 'stacked-animals' motif. On Sumba, and especially on Timor, either the creatures in the mother-*naga* group are all birds, or else the higher one is a bird and the one below is a *naga*. There are even examples of a quadruped standing on a bird. On Timor most of these figures appear on the handles of spoons made of horn.

25 The point of main interest in this for us is the fact that the 'stacked-animals' motif was at once typical of the Sarmatian branch of the Central Asian animal style (the Sarmatians were a mounted nation occupying the steppe between the Aral and the Caspian Sea, during the last centuries BC), **47** and a frequent feature of open-work bronze pieces from the Ordos Steppe. There are Ordos plaques with horses or stags stacked one above the other, spoons with the same thing as the handle and pendants consisting of a pony with a foal, or even two foals atop of each other, standing on its back. That the animals were horses in this area and *nagas* in Indonesia does not weaken the comparison for, as already pointed out, forms tended to be taken over but given a different content in a new cultural environment.

49 Spoons from Timor often have, in addition, the plaited band and pairs of birds with their necks crossed. The latter motif is a simplified form derived from birds with their necks intertwined, a motif that probably originates from the Middle East, where it appears frequently on Babylonian seals. A Sarmatian open-work piece found in northern China displays an intermediate form in which the intertwining of the necks is scarcely recognisable and they simply cross over. With such extensive similarities there is good reason to trace the mother-*naga* of Borneo, Timor and Alor and the stacked animal figures back to mounted nomad art.

The scroll-*naga*, which only appears on Alor, may conceivably be derived from the same source as well. Some Siberian bronzes have an animal head looking as though it

were surrounded by antlers, but on examination the antlers resolve themselves into hook-like birds' heads attached to the animal's head in a completely non-organic manner. The scrolled 'foliage' attached to the Alor *nagas* usually bears a marked resemblance to these birds' heads. Carved hunting scenes from the Mongolian-Chinese border area featured highly stylised and intertwined dragons, which may also have served as models for the scroll-*nagas*. They have the same attempted symmetry at both ends as in the Alor design. The prototypes of this *naga* may not be quite so obvious as for some others, but from what we can deduce about the diffusion of the Central Asian animal style in Indonesia, there is a strong probability that the source was the same.

Historical proof of these influences is still lacking and we have to rely on stylistic comparison, but it is possible to detect the effect of the nomad style reaching beyond eastern Indonesia perhaps as far as western Melanesia (New Guinea), but no further. Remembering the diffusion of the harpoon, briefly sketched on pages 45–46, we can recognise a zone, extending as far as Polynesia, the Marquesas islands and New Zealand, which has been open to the influence of prehistoric Eurasian and Sino-Siberian hunter and fisher cultures. The picture can be filled in by taking a geographical view of the comparison of axe-types, or of abstract artistic motifs like the spiral and the plaited band, which we have traced all the way from Mesopotamia to the Pacific Ocean.

The resemblance between Maori polished spirals (including those on nephrite axe-heads) from North Island, New Zealand, and archaic Chinese decorative forms is clear to see. Tattoo patterns and designs on carved bowls from the Marquesas also invite comparison with early Chinese ornamentation. The probable course of indirect influence from Han dynasty China through the archipelagoes of Oceania will be marked out in the following chapter on 'Circumpacific' art.

51. **Underside of a carved wooden bowl from the Marquesas islands.** W. 9½ in. (24 cm.). Museum für Völkerkunde, Munich. In this outpost of Polynesia, over 3000 miles from Central America, a strong, geometrical style of abstract decoration developed which forms a link between the art of China in the Chou period (1st millennium BC) and the art of pre-Columbian America. The design on this bowl is based on a stylisation of the squatting ancestor figure.

'CIRCUMPACIFIC' ART

The elements that go to make up the art of the Pacific islands are all found in the art of the Far East, and even if they were not transmitted directly by the high culture of China, they were all subjected to strong Chinese influences. China's role, both as the recipient and transmuter of Central Asian nomad motifs and as the agent of change among the more primitive cultures that lay around her, was a very active one and is an example of the multilateral traffic and interaction between cultures at different levels of advancement that was mentioned on pages 10–13.

The development of Chinese art during the first millennium BC was constantly affected by the art of the nomads, which eventually spread through various channels (one of them was the Dongson culture) to Indonesia and contributed to the formation of the ornamental-fanciful style in early Bronze and Iron Age art in this region. By exploring the trail of certain motifs, as was done on pages 79, 80 and 97, the movements of mounted nomad influence can be plotted on the map. Far-flung as this influence is, it was really only carried as far as the horse went—further progress was barred by the Sahara in Africa and the open sea in South-East Asia—and its spread does not nearly match the diffusion of the early farmer culture of South-East Asia.

The ancestor-worship of the farmer cultures and an over-riding concern with the increase of fertility found expression in the specific motif known as the 'squatting figure', and a variety of interrelated religious and cosmic concepts are bound up with its manufacture, design and purpose. The squatting figure is the basic motif of the art which is common to eastern Indonesia, Melanesia, northwest and Central America, and its derivative, the 'bent-knees' figure, is also the basic motif of Polynesian and of African art.

The style-structure of Oceanic art will be seen to lead us to a definition of 'Circumpacific' art, that is to say, a distinct art of the Pacific lands in the area extending from the seaboards of the Far East to the west coast of America, and eventually to East Africa, and including all the islands of Melanesia and Polynesia. Circumpacific art, which had quite important consequences for pre-Columbian American and for African Negro art, was thus of Asian origin— the mounted nomad style from the Eurasian steppes, and the early agriculturalist style from the Middle East.

We do not know who the first inhabitants of the Pacific Ocean islands were, but the latest archaeological finds and radio-carbon datings make it certain that by about the time of Christ the Polynesians must already have reached even an outlying group like the Marquesas. The Melanesians must have populated the archipelagoes we call Melanesia at a much earlier period—during the first millennium BC. The Polynesians and the Melanesians followed an agricultural way of life, with some hunting and fishing. Long before migrating to Oceania they had been skilled seafarers with an advanced boat-building technique. Although they had no metal, the shape of their stone axes shows signs of a recollection of metal forms which seem at some stage in their history to have been translated back into stone.

When the Polynesians settled in their islands, at a time corresponding to the Han period in China, they brought with them artistic motifs in a distinctly Chou style. In the course of time, these were modified and often turned into abstract patterns. Ripples of their culture certainly reached the American continent. Masks are an Oceanic speciality and their influence appears strongly in the Eskimo and Indian masks of the north-western coast. Easter Island often features prominently in discussions about the movement of cultural influences between South America and Oceania. Although it may also have been visited by people from Peru, as Thor Heyerdahl maintains, Easter Island's art is quite Polynesian in context and style. The famous stone figures are, in fact, perfectly typical bent-knees figures such as are found throughout Polynesia.

Motif and Variation

ANCESTOR WORSHIP

This basic motif in the art of the megalithic early farmer peoples of South-East Asia, and of late Neolithic mankind generally, arises out of ancestor worship, a system of beliefs and ritual in which the only object of worship are the spirits of a person's own departed forebears. The longer they are dead, however, the more god-like do human ancestors themselves tend to become in the petitioner's mind. The whole of life is thought to be lived under the watchful eyes of the spirits of the dead, and absolute conformity is the law for the living. The spirits insist that all must be carried on just as it was in their lifetimes and the possibility of change or progress in the community is almost excluded.

As the dead ancestors' wish is supposed to be eternal continuation in the living world through their offspring, human fertility becomes the centre of interest, and the means of transmitting the community's 'life-power' from generation to generation. This leads the individual to seek ways of gaining as large a share as he can of this 'life-power', and all spiritual power being thought of as concentrated in the head, the step is taken toward head-worship and, logically, toward head-hunting. For if you believe you can accumulate spiritual power by having the heads of other people in your possession, you start to collect them.

In South-East Asia, where the ancestor cult reached its fullest development, ancestors were very often represented by squatting figures in stone, and the carving of squatting figures in wood has been continued into modern times. The position is symbolic both of the foetus and of the mother giving birth, and expresses the early agriculturalist's preoccupations: fertility and life after death. It had forerunners in late hunter art of the Maglemosian period in northern Europe. A genealogical pattern pricked in a reindeer antler about 7000 BC shows the stylised figure of an ancestor at the root of the 'family tree', with the legs curved to suggest a squatting posture—possibly to symbolise the clan-mother giving birth.

The single squatting figure was not worked out fully as a motif until the food-producers came on the scene. They gave it the form that found general acceptance among primitive people who were at this stage of cultural development. The creation of the prototype for seated or squatting ancestor figures is associated with the early development of agriculture in southern China. The basic concept is not easy to define in a few words and needs to be approached through a network of related but distinct ideas. One of these was expressed in the widespread custom of burial in a crouched posture. This was certainly not in an attempt to bind up the dead and so prevent their return as ghosts, as was once suggested, but was a copy of the embryo position, to ensure their rebirth or at any rate to represent the belief in rebirth that the people held. From this to the representation of deceased ancestors in the same posture was for them a simple step.

South-East Asia (Burma, Thailand, Vietnam, Laos,

52 (right). **Copy of a Mesolithic ancestor-pattern from Denmark, pricked on a reindeer antler.** Maglemosian period, *c.* 7000 BC. See the text on this page.

53 (below). **Five carved wooden Batak 'magic wands' from Sumatra.** Full h. (from l. to r.) 67 in. (170 cm.), 46 in. (117 cm.), 65 in. (165 cm.), 58¼ in. (148 cm.), 55 in. (140 cm.). Museum für Völkerkunde, Munich. Despite the limited possibilities of treatment offered by these staves, they are carved in a compact and monumental style worthy of sculpture on a larger scale, expressing the symbolic heaviness of objects laden with the accumulated 'spirit power' of the ancestors.

52

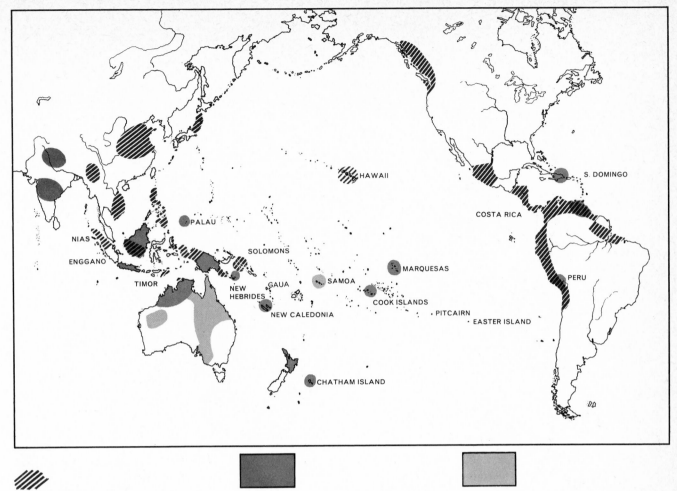

Area of diffusion of explicit squatting figures (mainly sculpture)	Area of diffusion of fertility representations based on the squatting figure	Area of diffusion of abstractions of the squatting figure

**39,41,
42**

Cambodia), Indonesia, the Philippines and Melanesia as far as the central Solomon Islands form the primary area in which squatting figures of ancestors are most frequently found, but we can see that the motif spread to more distant areas. By-passing Polynesia, where art is dominated by an attenuated variant known as the 'bent-knees' figure (this will be discussed in a later section), it recurs distinctly and plentifully in North-West America, Mexico (Guerrero State), Guatemala, Costa Rica, Colombia and Venezuela.

I

**H;46
47**

THE DIFFUSION OF THE 'SQUATTING FIGURE'

The Djarai tribe of southern Annam produce both explicit sculptures of the squatting figure and lozenge-shaped stylised patterns based on the same motif. The Wa tribe in Upper Burma use squatting figures carved in wood as receptacles for the heads of their victims (see page 122). The chief source in Indonesia is Borneo, where the motif is worked in the round, in relief and in textiles. The carved figures are generally embellished with a protruding tongue and occasionally with antlers as well—two special attributes of an evil-averting image. Even when the Borneo artists tended to lose sight of the original form of the squatting figure motif in their carvings and textiles, the presence of the male genitals usually remained as a reminder of the ancestor-worship concept in the background. The only examples in Sumatra are found sporadically among the Batak tribe in the northern part of the island, who set up

68,69

70

squatting figures in stone on their large burial cists and carved them in wood on various household objects and on their genealogical 'magic wands', which are of interest as evidence of the diffusion of another prehistoric motif (see page 131). Nias and Enggano, two of the chain of islands lying off the west coast of Sumatra, provide other examples. On Nias, which is notable for its wealth of megalithic monuments, the motif pervades the numerous wooden carvings on the island. Ancestor figures appear in a variety of postures, squatting, seated and standing, nearly always explicitly male and sometimes wearing elaborate and faintly antler-like headgear.

53

71,72

The motif has been found cast on a prehistoric bronze axe-head from Roti, off Timor. On Babar, Tanimbar and Leti Islands in the Banda Sea the figure takes on a particularly unambiguous and tyrannical appearance. (The Leti figures have affinities with the types both in Upper Burma and in western New Guinea). The most common form on Sumba, between Timor and Java, is in textiles. Other examples from the Banda Sea and Arafura Sea area are found on Wetar Island and the Kai and Aru groups. A special elaboration of the squatting figure is encountered in New Guinea, where it may serve (as among the Wa of Upper Burma) as a skull-holder or *korvar*, about which more will be said later when we consider the close connection between ancestor worship, head worship and head hunting. The parts of New Guinea where the squatting

38,54

54. Carved wooden ancestor figure from Babar island, Indonesia. h. 4¼ in. (11 cm.).

55. Batak stringed instrument from Sumatra. h. 23½ in. (60 cm.). Both Museum für Völkerkunde, Munich. The megalithic tradition in Indonesia is represented by the wooden squatting ancestor figures carved in the round in a style derived from the stone sculpture of the early farming cultures in the area. The Babar island figure (see also plate 38) shows the basic form, to which the Batak artists imparted their stronger sense of design.

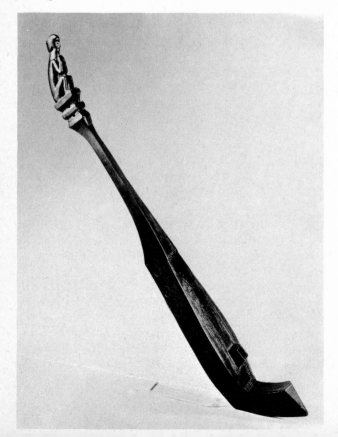

figure occurs are on Geelvink Bay, in the Massim district and on the Torres Strait coast, and further east, also in New Georgia and Shortland Island in the centre of the Solomon Islands group. The formerly headhunting Igorot tribe in the mountains of northern Luzon in the Philippines carve figures in both the distinct and the derived forms which display similarities with the types from eastern Indonesia and Upper Burma.

THE ORIGIN OF THE SQUATTING FIGURE

The earliest anthropomorphic figures shown in a recognisably squatting posture have been found painted on Chinese Neolithic pottery of the Yang Shao period (about 2200–1700 BC). They seem to have an ancestor-cult significance, although the motif had not at this stage acquired its later standard form. One figure has its hands raised and elbows bent, and its legs in a peculiar position—the knees seem to be splayed outward—but the figure as a whole easily suggests a naked man squatting on the ground. Another version, with a heavy circle for its head, has the hands pointing downward and parallel lines at right-angles to the backbone, presumably representing the protruding ribs of a dead man's corpse. A frog-like design also appears on Yang Shao pottery, alternating with these schematic human figures, and eventually merging with them. The symbolism of the frog has been discussed by Hanna Rydh in connection with a very ancient representation on a vessel from Susa of about 4000–3600 BC:

59a

60a

59b

> ...the frog or lizard whose symbolical character of denoting the uterus is testified of by many investigators. Should the frog be regarded as a symbol of rain, in the same way as the axe is said to represent Thor's thunderbolt, this must no doubt imply a secondary development, and primary symbolism of promoting fertility will also have survived. We see the frog symbol, together with the triangular and comb ornaments, on a Susa vessel, as well as on a remarkable Thuringian vessel of the Halstatt period.

(Continued on page 121)

58 (opposite). **Centreboard of a raft from Peru** (detail). Ica style, c. 1200–1400 AD. Wood. Full h. 5 ft. 11 in. (180 cm.). Museum für Völkerkunde, Munich. Until the Dutch introduced the centreboard into Europe from the East Indies, the only parts of the world where this device was known were S.-E. Asia and on Lake Titicaca in Peru (as recounted in Thor Heyerdahl's *Kon Tiki*). Dropped through the centre of a raft, a centreboard could make a raft manageable in open water. The decoration of this finely-worked ancient Peruvian example has striking parallels with models in Oceania, thousands of miles away, linking it with a source in Asia. The squatting figures on top (they seem to be the row of dancers variant) suggest Melanesian style. The fore-edge displays segments of the step and fret motif (plate 40) which is derived from the spiral meander.

59 (left). **Carved door-post from New Caledonia,** Melanesia. Late 19th century. Wood. h. 5 ft. 5½ in. (166 cm.). Museum für Völkerkunde, Munich. A compact version of the ancestor figure merged with a 'genealogical tree' in which the squatting forebears on the trunk have been reduced to an abstract pattern.

60 (below). **Painted shoulder cape of the Chilkat Indians,** Nootka, Vancouver Island, British Columbia, Canada. Before 1850. Woven cedar bark and goat's wool. l. *c.* 5 ft. (1.5 m.). British Museum, London. Humour and formal inventiveness distinguish this modern continuation of the X-ray style (see plates 11, 12). The Chilkats' blankets or capes are ceremonial robes worn only by chieftains and sometimes by shamans, although not for religious purposes.

61 (opposite). **Mask from Saibai Island,** Torres Strait, Papua. Probably early 20th century. Wild plum wood, shells, grass and fibre. h. 28½ in. (72.5 cm.). Royal Scottish Museum, Edinburgh. Worn for the celebration of the wild plum harvest, this rare Melanesian mask achieves its expressive effect by a clever use of materials and decorative forms.

62 (above). **Maori carving.** Early 19th century. Wood. h. 6¼ in. (16 cm.).

63 (above). **Ancestor skull with clay modelling from New Britain,** Melanesia. 19th century. h. 11 in. (28 cm.).

64 (below). **Ancestor skull with spirals from New Zealand.** Late 19th century.

h. 6¾ in. (17 cm.). 62, 63, 64 from Museum für Völkerkunde, Munich.

65 (below). **Mask representing an old woman of the Niska tribe,** upper Nass river, British Columbia, Canada. 1825–1850. Wood. h. 9½ in. (24 cm.). Museum of the American Indian, New York. The skulls and masks illustrated on

these two pages represent various stages of development of an artistic theme that stems from the head worship of prehistoric farming peoples in S.-E. Asia, which is discussed in the chapter *Motif and Variation.*

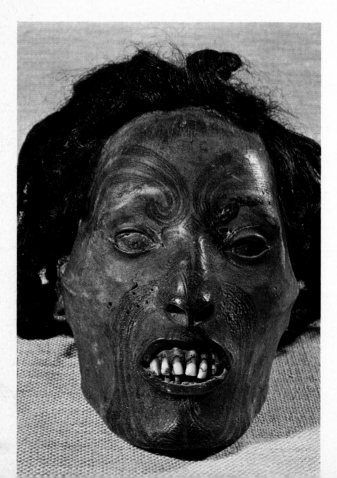

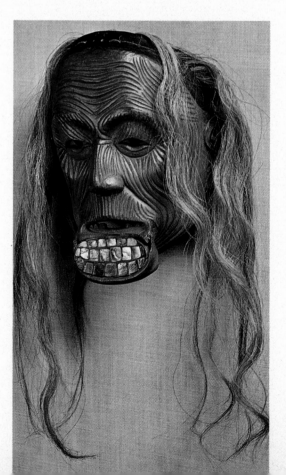

66. **Ancestor skull with modelling from Gaua Island,** Banks group, New Hebrides, Melanesia. End of the 19th century. h. 11¾ in. (30 cm.). Museum für Völkerkunde, Munich. The realistic modelling in clay on the dead man's own skull keeps the idea of his personality alive among the people.

67 (left). **Ancestor skull with modelled features from the Sepik River Valley,** New Guinea. Early 20th century. h. 6 in. (15 cm.). Museum für Völkerkunde, Munich.

69 (opposite, left). **Shield from the Sepik River Valley,** New Guinea. Early 20th century. Wood. h. 5 ft. 5 in. (165 cm.). Museum für Völkerkunde, Munich. Two impressive specimens of Sepik valley style (plates 32, 43, 73) which display several basic motifs charted in this book. Traditional spirals are sensuously drawn in white earth over the red clay modelling on the ancestor's skull with its effective cowrie-shell eyes, while the grotesque design of a face on the shield sticks out its tongue in an evil-averting gesture which has been traced back to early farming cultures in southern China.

68. **Figure for warding off spirits of disease from the Nicobar Islands.** 19th century. Wood. h. 3 ft 5 in. (1.04 m.). British Museum, London. The squatting posture shows very clearly in this protective image, placed at the village entrance (compare with plate 53), from islands in the Indian Ocean. The motif must have been carried to Madagascar by migrants from this side of the Ocean.

70 (below). **Prow ornament from the Solomon Islands,** Melanesia. Late 19th century. Carved wood with mother-of-pearl inlay. h. 7 in. (18 cm.). Museum für Völkerkunde, Munich. Almost African Negro in feeling, these were typical adornments of boats used on head-hunting expeditions. With its rhythm thrusting down and ahead the figure seems to be cutting the waves like a canoe's prow. The face is carved to resemble clay modelling on an ancestor skull and the glittering mother-of-pearl inlay represents tattooing. The pierced ear-lobes would also have been inlaid.

71 (opposite). **Mask from the New Hebrides, Melanesia.** Early 20th century. Bark, bast and clay. h. 35½ in. (90 cm.). Museum für Völkerkunde, Munich. Inspired by the clay-modelled skulls of ancestors, masks in the same style came to be made for dancing in, to represent the spirit of the dead man. When worn in movement, the great three-pronged headdress would sway impressively.

72. **Long-peaked Aleut hunting hat from Alaska.** *c.* 1850. Painted wood, incised ivory, beads and sea-lion whiskers. h. 8¾ in. (22.3 cm.). Museum of the American Indian, New York. These unique and fanciful hats served a useful purpose: like the peak of a sporting cap, they shielded the chiefs' eyes from dazzle at sea as they led the hunt in their boats. The compact spiral decoration provides a link with the Amur peoples across the Bering Straits in N.-E. Asia. (The bead-topped crown has a distinctly Mongolian air). The waving sea-lion whiskers were to give the wearer magic protection and ensure the success of the hunt.

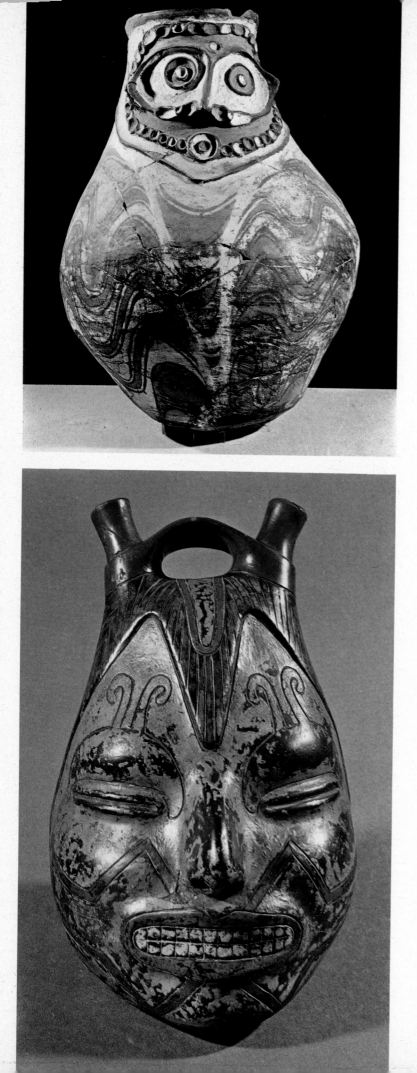

73 (left, above). **Face urn from the Sepik River Valley,** New Guinea. 19th century. Clay. h. 25½ in. (65 cm.). Museum für Völkerkunde, Munich.

74 (left, below). **Vessel in the shape of a trophy head from Paracas,** Peru. 1st–5th centuries. Clay. h. 8¾ in. (22 cm.). Museum für Völkerkunde, Munich.

75 (opposite). **Mask of the Mixtec culture from near Tilantongo,** Oaxaca, Mexico. *c.* 1200 AD. Wood covered with mosaic of turquoise, mother-of-pearl and pink shell. h. 6 in. (15.5 cm.). Robert Woods Bliss Collection, National Gallery of Art, Washington. In primitive cultures all round the Pacific, the mask continued the head-worship concepts that underlay the veneration of ancestors' skulls and the consequent custom of head hunting. In widely separated areas, vessels shaped like human heads—such as the example in Sepik Valley style and the other, more sophisticated one from a mature pre-Columbian culture in South America—were clearly substitutes for captured trophies. The same sense of awe for the human countenance dominates them both, as well as the Mixtec mask. Jade or turquoise mosaic inlay work was developed to great perfection by the Central American high cultures (Mixtec, Toltec, Aztec, Maya), among whom primitive agriculturalist ideas were nevertheless preserved and even exaggerated, right up to the Spanish conquest (1519–20).

76 (above). **Turquoise pectoral ornament of the Mixtec culture,** Mexico. 14th–15th centuries. l. 18 in. (46 cm.). British Museum, London.

77 (below). **Painted fabric of Chimú style from a tomb at Chanchan, Peru.** 1200–1400 AD. h. 4 ft. 1½ in. (126 cm.). Museum für Völkerkunde, Munich. The 'snake of heaven', with a head at both ends, is a motif that crossed the Pacific from southern China (plate 22) *via* Melanesia and is found in North, Central and South America. Compare the Mexican mosaic inlay work of plate 75 with plate 76.

78 (opposite). **Head of the Maya maize god from Copán,** Honduras. *c.* 1100. Stone. h. 27½ in. (69.7 cm.). Robert Woods Bliss Collection, National Gallery of Art, Washington. The god in this famous sculpture from the façade of Temple 26 at Copán, personifies the fertility of plants. Common to all the farming peoples from Asia to America, the representation reaches its height of artistic expression in the high cultures of Central America. This mastery over the sculptor's material evokes comparison with the introspective Buddhas of South-East Asia.

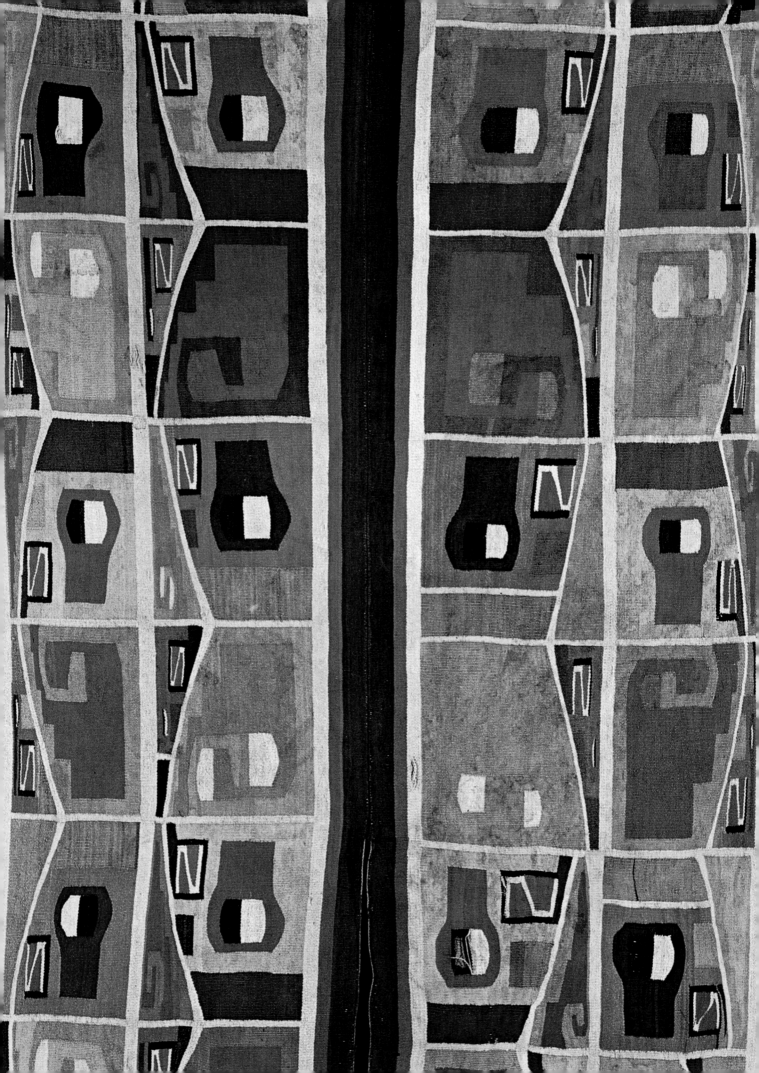

The inscriptions on early bronzes frequently contain pictograms showing a squatting figure together with a frog. The great Swedish sinologist Bernard Karlgren once observed, when two characters at the side of one of these representations had been read for him as *tsi min*, 'son-frog', that this 'makes little sense'. In fact, as we shall see, the sense is almost certainly right. The Chinese scholar Li Chi has pointed out that the ancient meaning of the forms and symbolism of early Chinese bronzes can often only be elucidated with the aid of the surviving traditions of primitive peoples on the southern fringe of Chinese civilisation. Now the Wa people of Upper Burma—head-hunters with definite squatting figure sculpture in wood—say they are descended from an ancestral frog, so that early Chinese characters reading 'son-frog' could easily refer to a creation myth once held in common, in which mankind was seen as the children of the frog.

Li Chi has also noted that prior to the beginning of the Shang era, at the end of the Neolithic in China, an east-coast people belonging to the black pottery Lung Shan culture were known as the 'Eastern I' or 'Squatting Barbarians', one of two peoples who may possibly have been the forerunners of the Shang dynasty. Li Chi observes, 'the founders of the Shang dynasty were probably the earliest Chinese who developed the kneeling posture into a sitting habit, known later among the Japanese as *seiza*.'

By the time we get to the white ware of the Shang period, the figure has gone the way of most motifs in Chinese art during this time, and it is dissolving into abstract patterns. The position of the arms, however still enable us to recognise the original shape. A late Shang or early Chou bronze has one of the same kind. The figure was also subjected to the 'split-profile' treatment, from one half of which the later squatting figures in profile were to grow. The first of these appears on a Chou bronze. The little carved stone squatting figure excavated near Anyang in the Shang dynasty capital has already been mentioned on page 75. The latest examples are found on terracotta tomb-facings of the Han period (206 BC–220 AD) and thereafter the motif seems to have faded out of Chinese art.

The evidence of these motifs continuing to be used by the primitive farmer peoples to the south and south-east of China confirms the supposition that they preserved almost unaltered the forms that were common to their own ancestors and to the early Chinese. It is likely that when the population pressure in the regions of southern China precipitated large scale migrations, the bearers of the various farming cultures spread out over Indonesia and Oceania in successive waves, taking their old motifs with them. The closeness of Marquesas patterns on carved bowls to the style of Chou period Chinese art is corroborated by the settlement of the islands about 200 AD, as has been established by H. L. Shapiro. Likewise, skeletal figures cut in the bark of trees on the Chatham Islands, east of New Zealand, in memory of the dead, are fairly direct continuations of the corpse-like ancestor figure noticed on

59c

38

51

60b

56. **Javanese kris.** Full l., 12¼ in. (31 cm.).
57. **Sumatran knife.** Full l., 19¼ in. (49 cm.). Both Museum für Völkerkunde, Munich. A squatting figure forms the hilt of both, but the difference in style between the two islands is marked.

58. Carved wooden ancestor figure from the Eilanden river, S.-W. New Guinea. h. 29¾ in. (75.5 cm.). Museum für Völkerkunde, Basle. The flowing lines of the arches formed by this lanky-limbed figure's joined elbows and knees are expressive of the decorative style of the New Guinea peoples, as seen in the lively designs carved and painted on their shields. The squatting posture is also a prototype for all Melanesian ancestor figures.

Yang-Shao painted pottery. These Chatham Island 'dendroglyphs' and a compact tattoo design from the Marquesas Islands are the purest and also the most distant derivatives of the motif as it was used in Neolithic China some 1500 years BC.

60c

HEAD-HUNTING, THE SKULL CULT AND *Korvars*

The extension of the belief in the head as the dwelling place of spiritual power to the practice of head-hunting has already been mentioned. Little as modern civilised man may sympathise with ideas that justify human sacrifice or the related custom of cannibalism, it is necessary, if we are to understand the nature of much of the art of primitive peoples, to recognise the importance that these essentially magical actions had for them. Throughout the area of early farming culture which is marked by the diffusion of the squatting figure motif, the ancestor image is repeatedly associated with the skull-cult, in a form known by the eastern Indonesian term *korvar*.

The *korvar* consists of a squatting figure with a human skull in place of the carved head, or with a skull inserted into a hollow head. They are ancestor figures offering a resi- dence to the spirit of the dead men whose skulls are affixed to them, and in this way making the latter's ghostly assist- ance available to the living owners of the *korvars*. The way this worked comes out clearly in a description of the Wa tribe of Upper Burma in an article by H. E. Kauffmann:

The head-hunting of the Wa is sheer fertility magic and is therefore undertaken before the spring sowing. Prayers are not offered to the captured heads for the enticement of the dead men's relatives so that they, too, should lose their heads to the victors (as is done among the Nagas). Instead, the heads receive ceremonial wor- ship and are ranked with the mighty spirits that can bring fruitfulness and prosperity. All members of the community bring them offerings... Each skull is placed inside a hollow wooden squatting figure, or in a square wooden chest, and these idols stand at the entrance to the village to ward off evil spirits, cattle-rustlers and disease. The primeval parents of the Wa, themselves descended from a frog, killed and ate another human being... The decomposing skull of this first victim of violence painted mysterious signs on the rock on which it lay, and these so pleased the highest spirit that he gave the two proto-Was sons and daughters. Ever since, it has been necessary to capture heads in order to ensure fertility for the Wa. In their myth of origin, cannibalism and head-hunting are intimately connected.

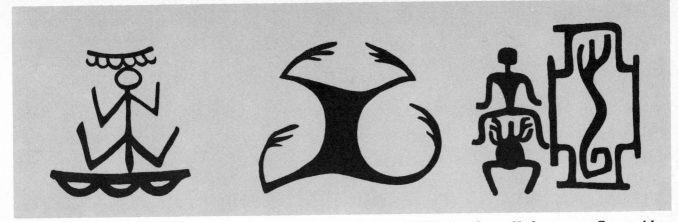

59 (above). **Earliest of the squatting figures from China.**
a. **Copy of painted decoration on Yang Shao ware**
(*c.* 2200–1700 BC).
b. **Copy of painted decoration (? frog) on Yang Shao ware.**
a and *b* after J. G. Andersson (see Further Reading List).
c. **Copy of tsi min ('son-frog') character, with adjacent
snake sign, on a Shang or Chou bronze vessel** *c.* 1500–1000
BC). After B. Karlgren (see Further Reading List).

60 (below). **Diffusion of a motif: the ancestor figure with
protruding ribs to indicate the spirit of a dead person.**
a. **Copy of painted decoration on Yang Shao ware** (*c.* 2200–
1700 BC). After J. G. Andersson (see Further Reading List).
b. **Tattoo pattern from the Marquesas Islands.** After
K. von den Steinen (see Further Reading List).
c. **Bark carving ('dendroglyph') from the Chatham
Islands.** After C. Jefferson (see Further Reading List).

61 (left). **Indonesian carved wooden
bowl supported by two squatting
figures from Sumatra.** h. 9½ in.
(24 cm.). Museum für Völkerkunde,
Munich. The squatting figure motif could
be put to many uses, and in this treatment
of an ancestral couple as supporters of a
large bowl the Indonesian artist exploited
the sculptural possibilities of the basic form
(figure 58) in a new and striking fashion.

63. **Batak wooden mask and hands.** h. of mask 13 in. (33 cm.). h. of hands 11 in. (28 cm.). Museum für Völkerkunde, Munich. It is not known for certain whether the hands were used by a dancer wearing the mask. The mask itself is an expressive variant of the skull and head motif.

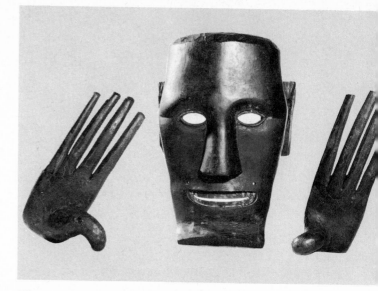

The wooden chests Kauffmann refers to are roughly-hewn and hollowed-out cubes of timber, into which the skulls are inserted. It is interesting that they are decorated with lozenge shapes, which frequently appear in the whole squatting figure area as an abstraction from an original form with the arms crossed in front.

The skull motif in Circumpacific art can be broadly defined as an over-emphasis of the head. In place of the custom of decorating the head-trophies of enemies taken in battle or of sacrificial victims (often these were the same) in southern China during the second millennium BC there arose the artistic substitute of carving heads in wood or stone. This introduced the beginning of figure sculpture in the Far Eastern, Pacific and African areas, where the earliest statues often exaggerate the size and features of the head. Ornamented human skulls are common in Borneo, New Guinea and New Zealand. Earthenware replicas of decorated heads are found in Peru. Evil-averting faces reduced to basic features, or to the eyes alone, are found on door-posts and shields in Borneo and New Guinea.

63,64
66,67,7

69

The face or mask motif, whether on its own, as in these instances, or as part of the squatting figure motif, has a precise meaning. It is to ward off evil. Its effectiveness was often thought to be enhanced by the typical protruding tongue, which is found in early examples in China and also in Borneo, Enggano and the Sepik River district in New Guinea. Another evil-averting or 'apotropaic' addition to the basically protective and increase-inducing squatting figure takes the form of antlers, or of the vestiges of what were once antlers, on the head. Such figures are found on Nias Island, in Borneo and on Leti Island in eastern Indonesia, and, like the squatting figure itself, its origin is certainly Chinese. The antler and tongue motif has been traced back to the second millennium BC in South China by Alfred Salmony (see the Reading List).

The huge *wondjina* rock pictures in north-western Australia are a naive version of the ancestor-skull motif, and for once unconnected with head-hunting. *Wondjina*

62. **Melanesian carving in tree-fern pith of an ancestor figure with two heads from Banks island,** New Hebrides. h. 71 in. (180 cm.). Museum für Völkerkunde, Basle. An ancestor tree of 'stacked' figures simplified to a pair of superposed faces. The porous tree-fern pith hardens in the air.

designs are based on the shape of a skull lying on its side, *minus* its lower jaw, and the skulls of dead members of the group, painted with red ocre, are laid at the foot of all rock faces on which *wondjinas* appear. Archaic as their style makes them seem to be, *wondjinas* are in fact quite recent and probably due to a Melanesian influence.

67, 63   Masks may be derived from the skull motif. In New Guinea, New Britain and the New Hebrides, masks began as the skulls of ancestors with human features modelled over them in clay, and were then elaborated into fantastic shapes. Melanesian mask-making did not spread to Polynesia (any more than the proper squatting figure did) **65**   but clearly reached North America and the western Eskimos, and took luxuriant root in Africa.

The variants of the *korvar* are divided into a standing (Indonesian) and a squatting type. There are plain figures and others holding out various attributes in their hands, such as a shield, or rods which sometimes join up in a sort of railing and at others are identical with rigid snakes. The association of an ancestor figure with snakes is far from surprising when we remember the early example of the **59c**   'son-frog' characters next to a snake on the Shang or Chou bronze from the Wessén Collection. The *korvars* holding perpendicular rods in front of them also call to mind an initiation ceremony dance among the Aranda tribe of central Australia. Holding poles in front of them, the dancers who represent the spirits of slain and devoured members of the tribe re-enact their going in search of their killers. The circular patches painted on the dancers' bodies symbolise the dead men's skulls. A complex of ideas relating the squatting ancestor figure to cannibalism and the skull cult evidently meet and combine in the figures of the 'rod-korvars'. It is by no means a remote possibility that the **65**   famous Tahitian mourning garments, with their large discs of mother-of-pearl which may (like the Australian aborigines' round patches of paint) represent the skulls of the dead, are a product of the same ideas.

65 (above). **Polynesian ceremonial garment worn by the chief mourner at burial rites in Tahiti.** British Museum, London. See the adjoining text.

Varieties of 'genealogical tree' from Sumatra to the Marquesas.

66. Upper part of a Batak 'magic wand' from Sumatra. Full h. 67 in. (170 cm.). Museum für Völkerkunde, Munich. A back view shows how the figures interlock with a characteristic compactness of handling (see plate 36).

67. Polynesian wooden carving of the god Tangaroa from Rarotonga, Cook islands. h. of whole shaft, 28½ in. (72 cm.). Museum für Völkerkunde, Munich. Turned on its side, the pegs become a row of squatting deities alternating with bat-like creatures.

68. Carved wooden handle of a fan from the Marquesas Islands, Polynesia. h. of whole fan, 17¾ in. (45 cm.). Museum für Völkerkunde, Munich. The stylisation of the figures touches on playfulness.

BEAR MAGIC

A special type of squatting figure sculpture occasionally appears in some areas in the guise of a bear, and this is undoubtedly an extremely ancient, and perhaps even the most ancient form, going back to early hunter concepts. It may be that the ancestor cult of the early farmers absorbed existing traditions from the old bear cult of the hunters, which found expression in the original squatting figures. The farmers' skull-cult, for example among the Nagas of Assam, involved prayers to the spirits in the captured heads that they might call their relatives to come and suffer the same fate at the victors' hands. The same idea inspired the Siberian hunters' bear-magic down to the eighteenth century. They reverenced the corpse of the dead bear, asking its spirit to go home and tell the other bears how well it was being treated and advise them to come and join it here.

The Ainu of Hokkaido, southern Sakhalin and the Kurile islands, and the Gilyaks on the lower Amur in Siberia both practised the bear cult as recently as the beginning of the twentieth century. They would capture a bear cub for sacrifice, but would first raise it in the village with every attention. When fully grown the bear was killed in such a way as to spare it as much suffering as possible. These tribes did not, however, produce any noteworthy images of bears, as was the case in China, where the earliest version of the squatting figure as a bear was found at Anyang, dated about 1300 BC.

North-West American carvings and decorative art frequently exhibit squatting bears, both full-face and in profile. The bear enjoyed a central position in the mythology and the totemistic beliefs of these Indian peoples. Stylistic comparison points to Chou period China as the source of their squatting bear figures, although nothing is known for certain about the route by which the motif reached this part of America. A squatting figure resembling a bear occurs on the handles of Tahitian fans, and may be a stylised reminiscence of bear images on the Asian main-

53 land. Batak 'magic-wands' include a carved ancestor-tree made up of bears standing on all fours on each other's backs. The Batak would, of course, have known the local species of wild bear in Sumatra, *ursus malayensis*.

THE PROBLEM OF THE ROCK PICTURES

As squatting figures express the beliefs of a specific group of Stone Age farmers, they should have no place in the rock art characteristic of the early hunters. It is therefore at first somewhat surprising that rock pictures of squatting figures should be widespread in the Pacific area. The hunters themselves made a home in Australia, but they never colonised the islands of the South Seas. It seems that the farmers must have learnt the art of making rock pictures from the hunters, probably in Indonesia, and that they then carried it with them as they expanded eastward by sea.

Paintings and engravings of squatting figures on rocks begin on the island of Ceram in the Banda Sea, in eastern Indonesia, and extend to western New Guinea and the north-western coast of Australia and the interior of Western Australia, as well as among the Bnang in parts of eastern New Guinea. For the rest of the area of diffusion it is necessary to distinguish between paintings and engravings of squatting figures. Rock paintings occur in New South Wales, Victoria and New Zealand. Rock engravings occur on Aneityum in the New Hebrides, on New Caledonia, in the Marquesas, Hawaii, on Pitcairn and Easter Island. Rock engravings are also found in the American North-West, in the area of the Central American high cultures, and all along the northern coast of South America from Peru to the Guyanas.

A study of the rock pictures of western New Guinea made by Josef Röder brought the fact to light that the native people have one name (*mututo*) that covers certain rock pictures as well as small carved wooden figures regarded, in true hunter fashion, as 'lords of the beasts' or 'lords of the fishes', and to which they make offerings, and another name (*maru*) for the conventional squatting figures which are common to the islands of eastern Indonesia, and which were treated as ancestor images until the growing influence of Islam drove the cult underground, if not into extinction. It would seem, therefore, that *mututo* images were a heritage from an earlier stratum of culture which was taken over by the agriculturalists and mingled with their own ideas. Distinct squatting figures appear in the rock pictures, and offerings were made to them as if to hunting spirits.

The red-painted figures are probably a thousand years older than the black-painted ones, which date from about the seventeenth to the nineteenth centuries AD. The culture of the artists who made the earlier and the later groups was a Stone Age one in both cases. Comparisons with rock art in nearby Australia are intriguing, but the date sequences of the Australian pictures are still too uncertain for us to draw anything more than tentative conclusions yet. It is noticeable, however, that the earlier, red-painted New

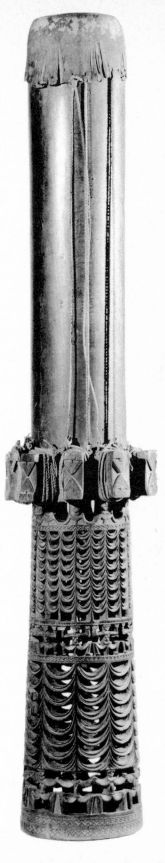

69. **Polynesian carved wooden drum from the Tubuai Islands.** h. 51¼ in. (130 cm.). Museum für Völkerkunde, Munich. The carved bands round the decorated base consist of rows of dancing girls. S. Polynesia, E. Australia and New Guinea (plate 50) are the only areas where this variant of the squatting figure occurs in which it is transformed into a figure in movement.

The 'bent-knees' figure in Indonesia
70 (far left). **Carved wooden house-post
from Borneo.** h. 55¼ in. (140 cm.).
Rietbergmuseum, Von der Heydt
collection, Zürich.
71 (left). **Carved wooden ancestor
figure from Nias island,** off Sumatra.
h. 11 in. (28 cm.). Museum für Völkerkunde, Munich.

Guinea rock pictures of squatting figures have many similarities with figures on rocks in north-western Australia.
These Australian squatting figures belong to a level that
lies between the preceding elegant small-figure style and
the *wondjina* style which comes down to the present day. If
we can date the red-painted figures in New Guinea around
1000 AD, the same era would be appropriate for the similar
squatting figures of the Kimberley ranges, Wonalirri and
Ngungunda.

In New Caledonia the rock pictures of squatting figures
are executed in a blurred and imprecise manner, but it is
possible to detect signs that they are intended to portray
figures in motion, a change which will be discussed in the
following section. The same applies to many of the rock
paintings found in New Zealand's South Island. (In North
Island there are plenty of carved reliefs of squatting
figures in wood, but, surprisingly, no rock pictures have
yet been found.)

CHANGED MEANINGS AND ABSTRACTION

Although the motif of the squatting figure and its derivatives have been handed down faithfully from generation to
generation for thousands of years and have spread round
the shores of the Pacific, providing a constant source of
inspiration for primitive artists wherever they were introduced, the content has been variable. The main kinds of
change which affected the basic figure—and each other—
were: the introduction of movement; the combination of
two figures in copulation scenes and of long rows of figures,
horizontally as dancers or, vertically as ancestors in
genealogical poles; the translation of the motif from the
round to two-dimensional forms; and, running through all
the foregoing, the tendency toward decorative abstraction.

In the following section on the special variant in Polynesia known as the 'bent-knees' figure we shall see how in
New Guinea the squatting figure had already begun to
evolve from a fertility-promoting ancestor figure to a man

72. Group of carved wooden ancestor figures from Nias island. h. 9¾ in. (25 cm.). Museum für Völkerkunde, Munich. All these examples of statues in the round with slight flexion of the legs come from an area where art is dominated by the motif of the fully squatting figure, of which it is a variant. Nias island, in particular, is rich in variants of the ancestor figure (71, 72). Only in Polynesia does the 'bent-knees' variant take over as the typical form of the image (see figures 73–79).

The roughly chipped sculpture from Borneo (figure 70) shows the megalithic style applied to wood and on the point of yielding to the ornamental-fanciful style (see figures 44–46) which reached Indonesia during the age of metal (see page 77). The phalluses emphasise the character of these figures as representations of ancestral spirits with an important fertility-promoting role.

in motion. By the time it reached the central Solomons, the new meaning was quite pronounced and from here, it probably spread to the rock pictures of New Caledonia, south-eastern Australia and the South Island of New Zealand. In other areas the older emphasis on fertility no doubt continued. The rock pictures of squatting figures certainly represent ancestors, as is evident in all examples from western New Guinea to South America.

Earlier in this chapter, we traced the origin of the ancestor figure in a squatting position back to Neolithic China and noted its ambiguous relationship to the frog-figure, with its fertility symbolism and its similarly displayed limbs. As the use of the squatting figure as a cult-image was spreading through South-East Asia, another seated figure with a not dissimilar meaning was spreading eastward from the Middle East through India to Indonesia. This was the female deity squatting with exposed pudenda which is known as the 'shameless woman' or 'nude goddess'

43

figure. The earliest examples come from Neolithic Egypt, and very numerous female figurines and other images in the toad or frog posture are found in India. The merging of the two prototypes seems to have taken place in Borneo, where the ancestor and fertility aspects were united in figural groups that included double-headed figures, sometimes expressing the duality of darkness and light, or the female and male principles, and sometimes stressing fertility with frank portrayals of copulation. These scenes are also found in north-western Australia and on some textiles from Peru. Derivatives in South America undergo a change of meaning, and the couples turn into pairs of figures with knees bent outward and representing 'culture heroes'— that is to say, particular ancestors who are remembered for having played an important part in the history of the group by inventing certain techniques or customs.

Another kind of change may be occasioned when sculpture is superseded by two-dimensional renderings.

44

73, 74 (below and right). **Polynesian carved wooden figure, called 'the god Te Rongo and his three sons', from Rarotonga,** Cook Islands. h. 27½ in. (69.9 cm.). British Museum, London. Cook islands style displays a regression from sculpture in the round toward two-dimensional forms (see figure 67). Even the figure in plate 52 is perfunctory in its physical details. This stylisation goes with a strong sense of formal qualities, expressed in almost nautical lines, befitting an aristocratic, seafaring culture.

There are, of course, squatting figures in the flat and in the minor arts at every turn in areas where three-dimensional sculpture predominates, but two-dimensional renderings are also found outside this area—and not just on the fringes, but far beyond them. They would seem to radiate from regions where sculpture flourishes into regions where there is none, or where it has died out.

In some areas of south-east Asia, particularly in Taiwan (Formosa) and its small neighbour Botel Tobago, two types of squatting figure are found in proximity of each other. There are firstly the derivatives of the common type, usually on reliefs, with the knees bent double, and secondly a version with the legs twisted upward. Is there a change in meaning between the two types? The answer, based on the evidence of the Asmat district in western New Guinea, seems to be that the second one represents a development of the first in a particular direction. In this area of relative density of squatting statues, and apparently in imitation of them we find figures carved in relief *in profile*, and then on shields. Here we are able clearly to trace meaning, interpretation and development: the squatting figure is no longer associated with the toad or frog, as made sense in Indochina, and perhaps also in Taiwan, where the ancient Chinese view of the frog as man's primeval ancestor lingered on. In southern New Guinea the squatting figure becomes a definite ancestor figure, then a protector in abstract form with evil-averting powers to be placed on shields, and finally a fertility figure.

In south-western New Guinea, in the Lorentz river area and the Asmat district, the squatting figure is flattened to two dimensions. This process is clearly evident and has several variants. At one time attempts were made to project the squatting figure in profile onto the plane but these attempts were apparently soon abandoned or else continued only in isolated instances. The following types

39,41,44 45,55,56 57

75 (left). **Polynesian carved stone figure from the Marquesas islands.** h. 8 in. (20 cm.). Museum für Völkerkunde, Munich. The precise Marquesan style turns sculptured figures into the static and formidable symbols of a society obsessed with warfare and social status.

were fully elaborated: frontal representation; frontal representation of a sequence of 'stacked' squatting figures (for example, on genealogical trees); representations of fertility scenes on the surface of shields, which then obtain **44** an evil-averting significance, which is shared by pictures of such shields.

The idea of a line of forebears crouching one above the other in a human tower may have led in later times to the carved ancestor poles that are widely disseminated in the *53,66* Pacific area. From the 'magic wands' of the Batak of Sumatra, through the Philippines, New Guinea, New *67* Ireland, New Hebrides, New Zealand, the Cook Islands *68* and the Marquesas to the giant 'totem poles' of north-western America, the pattern remains the same though the scale of the work and the interpretation of the object may *37* vary from place to place. Australian *tjuringas*, ancestor-poles from the Admiralty Islands and house-posts from South America are abstracted versions of the same thing. The individual figures making up an ancestor-pole are usually in a distinctly squatting posture, so that the idea of a tree of human generations was combined with the inherited conception of an ancestor figure. The scenes in the last class, and their abstract versions, are elaborately worked in south-eastern New Guinea, and from there seem to have been widely disseminated. Abstract copulation scenes, as for example on a shield from the Oba river (now in Djakarta Museum), are reduced to a pattern of parallel concavities, which as it runs through the ornamentation of southern New Guinea as far as the Gulf of Papua, becomes more and more abstract. In this ornamental form they were adopted for shield decoration in northern Queensland around the Gulf of Carpentaria, in central and southern Australia, and in patches in central Western Australia. On the Murray river, the pattern returns to a rather less abstract form. The whole family of these ornaments,

76. **Tangaroa at the moment of creating the other gods.** Polynesian carving in ironwood from Rurutu, Tubuai islands. 18th century. h. 44 in. (112 cm.). British Museum, London. On this unique and magnificent image of order forming out of chaos like an explosion of energy, new-born gods appear as squatting figures on the bent-knees figure of their creator.

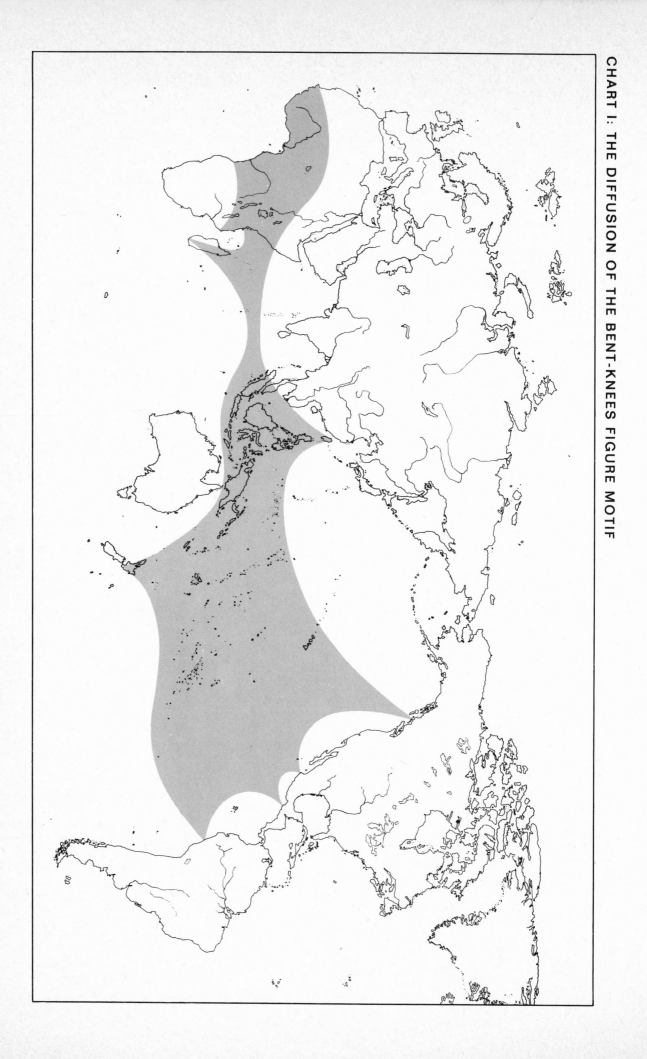

which David S. Davidson terms 'arches curved inward' grew from the abstract pattern evolved in the Asmat district of New Guinea.

Whereas in this development the original meaning is always adhered to, however abstract its external expression may become, a decisive change of meaning takes place in another development that also has its origin in New Guinea. This is the squatting figure represented in motion, which has a purely representational purpose. A bark-painting from the Aird river delta in New Guinea depicts a row of stylised squatting figures, which then turn into a row of dancers in headdresses and tailpieces, gesticulating, and stamping. Figurines in a similar posture, carved out of tridacna shells, are found on Choiseul Island in the Solomons. Their origin in ancestor figures is indicated by their use as gable-ends on small skull-treasuries. Some of the squatting figures in profile are, both in style and treatment, strikingly like the narrow-faced Cook Islands images of deities.

Squatting figures in motion are found in New South Wales and Victoria and in rock paintings in South Island, New Zealand, but principally in the decorative work of the Cook and Tubuai Islands. Cook Islands paddles are decorated with rows of squatting figures in a dancing movement. On Mangaia in the Cook Islands, there is an exception to the usual Polynesian myth of Tiki, the first man, which is relevant to the importance of these dancing figures. Uniformly throughout Polynesia, with only slight variants, the squatting figure is identified with Tiki, but on Mangaia Tiki is taken, for once, as the female principle and is thought of as the sister of the first man. So the transformation of the squatting (male) Tiki image into a distinctly female dancer on ceremonial paddles from Mangaia is understandable in terms of the local belief.

THE BENT-KNEES FIGURE

This curious variation of the ancient squatting figure, with its springy, almost stamping posture—as if the image is about to break into a tribal dance—is particularly interesting because of its very wide distribution through the world. Known to anthropologists as the 'figure with flexion of the legs', its derivation from the squatting type is so obvious that doubt can hardly arise. What is not so certain, however, is how the derivation came about.

Technical reasons are probably one cause. With the tools at their disposal—sharpened shells, coral or stone in Polynesia, and in bronze knives in Indonesia—it must have been less of a problem to carve the half-bent limbs without the hazardous undercutting necessary for a true squatting figure. Another reason seems to be a symbolic deduction from the meaning of the fully bent legs as representing life. In the creation myth of the artistically gifted, head-hunting Asmat people of south-western New Guinea, the creator descended from heaven by boat. He sailed down a river and on the way built a house which he filled with carvings of men and women, whom he then brought to life by the

77. **Polynesian carved female figure from Hawaii,** probably Pele, the volcano goddess. Wood with real hair and shell eyes. 18th century. h. 16½ in. (42 cm.). British Museum, London. The typical stance of the muscular legs poised for vigorous movement makes use of the bent-knees figure to reflect the well-known aggressive character of Hawaiian sculpture.

music of drums. Thus if squatting figures of ancestors represented them as alive, when made with straight legs they would represent ancestors who had not yet been brought to life. With bent knees they were therefore already almost alive. Finally, there is the aesthetic point that, as Sir Peter Buck points out, 'this attitude appears to give the figures more balance'.

The statue in the round with slight flexion of the legs appear, in the first place, in the same area as the squat statues proper: Borneo, the Philippines, New Guinea and the Solomons. The island of Nias provides examples of all the variants and developments, ancestor figures squatting, seated, and standing with bent knees or with straight legs. Most museums in the world have ample ancestor figures from Nias to illustrate developments from the original type.

Outside the area of the squatting statue proper, bent knees figures in the round are encountered on the Admiralty Islands, the New Hebrides, the Solomon Islands and New Caledonia. Throughout Polynesia, it is actually the normal type. 'One feature retained in common throughout Polynesia and New Zealand was the flexion of the legs', writes Sir Peter Buck, who has seen examples from Rarotonga, Aiutako, Tahiti, Raiavavae, the Marquesas, New Zealand, Mangarava, Easter Island, Hawaii and Tonga. It is a curious fact, however, that in this same area,

78. **Freestanding carved Polynesian figure of a man from New Zealand.** Wood with real hair. h. 15¾ in. (40 cm.). The Hunterian Museum, Glasgow. Unlike the silkily polished surface of the

Hawaiian figures to which they were related (figure 77), the Maori figures were ornamented more or less with spiral tattoo patterns derived from Chinese motifs of the Chou period (see plates 62, 64).

79. **Polynesian carved wooden ancestor figure from Easter Island.** h. 14½ in. (37 cm.). Museum für Völkerkunde, Munich. These figures are Polynesian in style but of a type only found on Easter Island.

the squatting figure proper appears but only in rock paintings, a point which was discussed on page 127.

The figure also occurs in relief carvings from the fringes of the squatting figure area—Siberia, southern Taiwan, Enggano, New Guinea, the Solomon Islands, New Zealand, North-Western America, and among the pre-Hispanic Arawaks both on Cuba and on the north-eastern coast of South America.

In Africa, as we shall see, the bent-knees figure is the standard posture of the ancestor figure in African art. After the mask (which can be traced to concepts similar to those that inspired the masks and skull motifs of the Pacific) the ancestor figure is the most frequent type in the whole of African sculpture. The link which shows the dependence of African sculpture on Indonesian prototypes is found in Madagascar, but much more research will be necessary before the process mentioned on page 163 can be fully described and documented.

In the previous section on rock pictures we saw that squatting figures in this form are widely diffused throughout the extensive areas of the Pacific where squatting figures in the round are never found. The reason for this is still a matter of conjecture, but it seems that the agriculturalist settlers of the Pacific Islands must somewhere have adopted the techniques of painting and engraving on

rocks from the old hunters. Rock art became the medium for ancestor figures in the squatting position, while the bent-knees variant replaced it entirely in sculpture in the round.

In New Caledonia the rock pictures featuring squatting figures are executed in a smudgy, imprecise style but the figures are clearly in motion. The paintings in the South Island of New Zealand also appear to be renderings of men in motion. In North Island there are numerous squatting figures carved in relief, but no rock pictures have yet been found there. The squatting figures of south-eastern Australia distinctly portray motion, both in renderings near Sydney and in western New South Wales. The only squatting figure in south-eastern Australia that definitely does not convey a sense of motion comes from the Coning Range rock shelter, Victoria. Extreme derivatives of squatting figures in the form of an inward curving arch, which may be derived from southern New Guinea (Papua), are encountered on implements, mainly shields, from Queensland down to Victoria. In the north-east, the squatting figures are almost wholly ornamental. Half-way down they merge with the rudimentary animal style, which came in from the north-west (Kimberley ranges), and in the south-east and south they are joined on the same object with the relatively free-flowing linear and geometric local style.

100,

93, 100

America

D

12
81
60

8

72

THE FIRST AMERICANS

Some scholars believe that man was already living in America twenty or thirty thousand years ago. We still have no certain proof of this, but it is at any rate now beyond doubt that he entered the American continent from Asia by way of the Bering Strait, bringing with him a definitely recognisable range of implements of the Magdalenian period at the latest. These included stone spearheads and the spear-thrower, which survived as a ritual object in the mature cultures of Mexico and Peru, and which is still used by the Eskimos for hunting. The X-ray style, so typical of the Magdalenian hunters and their descendants in northern Europe and northern Asia, also penetrated America from the north, but stopped short, for some reason, in Colombia and Venezuela. Traces of it survive to the present day in Eskimo and Pueblo Indian art. The cosmology of shamanism, which is connected with the X-ray style, was particularly highly elaborated among the Indians of North America.

A remarkable clue to the prehistoric migrations of the earliest inhabitants of America is provided by tracing a piece of hunting equipment, the harpoon. At the furthest point south they could possibly reach, Tierra del Fuego, a hunting culture is proved to have been in existence by bone harpoons comparable with one found at Ahrensburg, near Hamburg, and dated about 1200 BC.

The majority of early American rock pictures are animal representations, and the significance of the small percentage of human figures is therefore very great. In the Spanish Levant the combination of human and animal figures had been a later phase of the hunter peoples' rock art, the result of contacts with the newly-established urban cultures of the eastern Mediterranean, and although this Second Hunter style spread all through Africa, and traces of it reached South-East Asia and Australia, it hardly spread northward and certainly never crossed over to America at all. The inference, therefore, is that man's earliest hunter cultures in America developed from primeval food-gathering as a result of sea-borne influence from across the Pacific.

Primitive agriculture probably reached America by the northern route. The first crops cultivated were an early form of pumpkin (squash) and amaranth, a graminaceous plant which is known to have been growing in the Mississippi valley as early as 3000 BC. Amaranth was grown in Mexico, Guatemala, Peru, Bolivia and north-western Argentina in pre-Columbian times, and it is interesting to note that the same plant is cultivated in Persia, Afghanistan, south India, Ceylon, the Himalaya and western China.

Decorative forms of the art of the early farmers of Asia, such as the spiral, reached Alaska *via* the Bering Strait at about the time of Christ. Derivatives can be traced in the Punuk period (about 1000 AD) and finally in the simple circle and dot patterns of contemporary Eskimo art. Definite spirals are found across North America on the sites of a series of cultures: in the Hopewell stage in Ohio (about 500 AD), in the Swift Creek stage in Florida (about

80 (above). **Eskimo spoon from North America carved out of a walrus's shoulder joint.** 20th century. w. 2½ in. (6 cm.). Museum für Völkerkunde, Munich.

81 (below). **Tlingit Indian shaman's charm carved from an antler.** From the Sitka and Wrangell region, Alaska. *c.* 1825–75. l. 5 in. (12.7 cm.). Museum of the American Indian, Heye Foundation, New York. The Eskimos, who have survived in a bleakly uninviting habitat with enviable resourcefulness, still draw scenes which are parallelled in the rock art of Africa, Australia and the Spanish Levant. The Tlingit charm shows the influence of Chinese forms of the Chou period, especially in the frog-like heads of the spirit-helpers flying to the shaman's aid on the back of a winged snake. They are depicted with a psychological expressionism that is capable of arousing uneasy feelings even in a civilised beholder.

82. **Paumari Indian carved and incised wooden club from Amazonas,** Brazil. h. 35 in. (89 cm.). Museum für Völkerkunde, Munich. This elegant weapon from S. America has affinities not only with clubs of similar shape and decoration from the Massim area of New Guinea but also with the late Chou drumstand in plate 22, likewise decorated with a positive-negative spiral pattern.

500 AD), in the Anasazi culture in the South-West (about 500–1200 AD), in the Mississippi stage in Louisiana (about 1000–1300 BC) and on Caddoan style pottery in Arkansas (about 1400–1700 AD). The Naskapi people were using derivatives of the spiral ornamentally as late as the eighteenth century. Spirals are found in Mexico in Guerrero and Oaxaca states and at Cholula in Puebla state, and very distinct spirals decorated prehistoric objects found in Santo Domingo. The dissemination of the spiral in Central and South America seems independent of its spread in the northern part of the continent, and the pattern of distribution indicates that influences from the Pacific coast were at work here.

As we have seen, the other great agriculturalist motif from South-East Asia, the squatting figure, reappears strongly all along the west coast of America, although it is missing from Polynesian art. It is prominent in the minor arts of the North-West, in figures in the round among the Dakotas and in Florida, in architectural details in Central America, in the minor arts of the Mexican state of Guerrero and of Guatemala, in Venezuela and in pottery in Colombia. It is also found at Maracá and Marajó in the Amazon estuary. Derivative forms appear in the decorative arts of Peru. However, the American types of this motif were not as boldly depicted or as elaborately worked on as was the case in South-East Asia, nor did the American figures have such pronounced local differences. All give the impression of being more or less intermixed.

America thus received the already evolved and far from 'primitive' concepts of the Stone Age hunters of the Magdalenian epoch, who were followed by the early farmers. The migrations of these peoples took them and their cultures to America, but the curious feature about them is that once established in America, though they continued to receive and nourish stimuli from without, they made no further contribution of their own to world civilization. By themselves, they exploited all stimuli, concepts and motifs to the utmost limit—their achievement was often successfully to enlarge the *scale* of something—but it was the fate of the pre-Columbian peoples to remain isolated from human developments that were taking place in the rest of the world.

About 5000 BC the first settlements came into being. The majority still lived from primitive agriculture and hunting, but gradually great cultures began to grow in two regions. With the transition to organised agriculture there came the emergence of semi-urban cult-centres—about 1500 BC in Mexico and Central America, during the first millennium BC in the Andes, reaching their apogee between 300 and 900 AD. True cities did not develop in either region until shortly before the Spanish conquest, by which time the native cultures were already degenerating.

THE ART OF THE INDIANS

In a curious way, the art of the North American Indians generally fails to be properly understood by us. We tend to

83 (left). **Head of a carved wooden ceremonial staff from northern Brazil.** h. of staff, 44½ in. (113 cm.). diam. 1½ in. (3.8 cm.). Museum für Völkerkunde, Munich. The animal figure is covered with spiral decoration—a distant but clear echo of the mounted nomad style (see figures 38, 40).

84 (right). **Caddoan pottery water bottle from Quachita parish, Louisiana,** U.S.A. *c.* 1300–1700. h. 5¾ in. (14 cm.). Museum of the American Indian, Heye Foundation, New York. A classic example of Caddoan ware, this square-based vessel shows the preponderance of spiral ornamentation which was very marked in the prehistoric southeast. A comparison with Jōmon pottery from Japan (figure 35) is interesting.

have an entirely preconceived picture of their life and their art, which has become rooted in the average American's and European's consciousness. Largely to blame for this is the distorted image of the Indian in our myths of the West, which we absorb through film and story. Yet one of the original and greatest writers of the Western legend, James Fenimore Cooper, gives us the truest glimpse of the Indians and their world as it really was in the early Pioneer days.

Fenimore Cooper's wonderfully observed descriptions of the land and its people also convey something, the cause of which he cannot have understood as well as we can: the contrast between 'noble' hunters like the Delawares and the 'bloodthirsty' Huron. The Delawares were simple hunters, but the Huron were an offshoot of the continental farmer peoples and shared with the advanced cultures of Central America those agricultural fertility customs which were as incomprehensible as they were abhorrent to Europeans. But cruel rites are performed piously by primitive farming peoples all over the world and, like head-hunting and cannibalism, these customs are only in our time yielding their anthropological meaning to civilised mankind.

North American Indian Art is essentially a meeting of the unsophisticated hunter art of the far north, represented by the work of the Canadian Indians and the Eskimos (although ethnically distinct from the Indians, the Eskimos have for an immensely long time been the most primitive people on earth), with art on the periphery of the Central American mature cultures, represented by works found in the Mississippi basin and in the deserts of Arizona and New Mexico.

Eskimo and Indian hunter art is an extension of the hunter art of Northern Eurasia which gradually spread into North America across the Bering Strait or down the north-western coast. Well-authenticated dated objects from Alaska provide the evidence of this movement, and there is also the diffusion of specific motifs or styles to trace. The X-ray style is one of these, and from its first appearance in the Arctic art of northern Europe and Siberia it can be followed, through Eskimo art, all the way to New Mexico, where it was used on pottery by the Zuñi Indians, heirs of the Pueblo culture.

Animal-centredness is a characteristic of the hunter's mental make-up. Many Indian tribes expected the young men who were undergoing their initiation rites to train themselves to see certain visions. The ultimate object was to learn to produce an inner mental picture that would give one added strength. This was called a 'spirit helper' or 'medicine', and frequently took the form of an eagle or other creature. The animal-centred layer of consciousness was still very much alive.

Most examples of North American Indian art are now in museums, some having been collected by the settlers and adventurers of the past two centuries and the rest being the result of more recent scientific excavations on grave sites. The chief impression this art leaves on one is of a subtle and sophisticated sense of form. Ordinary objects of daily use often had such a mid-twentieth century look in their reduction to essentials that they might almost have come from the Knoll studios. Clay pipeheads, for example, were modelled with such a spare and monumental naturalism that they could be products of modern North America.

Even allowing for the possibility of a proportion of fakes finding their way into these collections, it is easy to see that a typically American 'sublimated' style runs right through the pottery, the painting and the basketwork.

The perfection of form was, however, easily lost and then one often feels a certain emptiness about the work, a remoteness from any central creative impulse. This remoteness was, of course, the North American Indians' greatest cultural drawback. The centres from which they drew their principal formative impulses were the hunter cultures of Siberia and the Central American farming cultures, both of which were a long way off.

The dilution of creative feeling in the more recent works of art—such as the Plains Indians' painting on hide and the modern silvercraft of the Pueblo Indians—coincided with the advance of European influence. The well-known sand pictures of the Navaho Indians, on the other hand, have remained untouched by European influences. Deriving from Central American ideas, and drawn in a very diluted and mechanical style on the ground with sand of various colours, the pictures play a part in religious ceremonies and are swept away when these have been concluded. The ceremonies still enshrine ancient concepts and the purpose of the sand pictures, which is to heal sickness, is still believed in by the Navahos. Sicknesses are treated with appropriate herbs and the god associated with a herb's particular myth is meanwhile represented in the design of the sand picture. Then, while chanting creates a state of

suggestion in his mind, the patient is carried to the picture, laid over it and given a medicinal plant brew to drink.

Traditional chants of the native peoples which have been collected over the years show that local styles of poetry and song corresponded in feeling with styles in the visual arts. Among the Eskimos there is a strong individuality and freedom of form. Among the settled peoples of the South West—the Pueblo Indians and, most of all, the Navahos—there is a rather abstract, refined and rarefied style, conditioned by the vast open spaces of the deserts and mountains where they live. 'Rarefied' does not necessarily mean a weak style but one that, like the atmosphere at a high altitude, is thin and cold. This effect is clearly seen in the art of Peru, in the highlands of the Andes.

The primitive hunting existence of the North American Indians was probably more successful, in its harmony of a simple life at one with nature, than that of any other similar group in the world. Their austerity, joined with artistic and religious intensity, found expression less openly in their art than in the fragments of their oral literature—including the reminiscences of some of the Plains Indian chiefs published in modern times—that have been preserved.

The relationship between the primitive Indians of South America and the high cultures of Peru is not yet well understood. This is partly because there has been far too little thorough investigation of the peoples who still exist, as they did at the time of the Conquest, at a level of culture that is generally half-way between hunting and farming. Decora-

85 (opposite, far left). **Warrior effigy pipe bowl from the Spiro mound,** Le Flore county, Oklahoma, U.S.A. *c.* 1200–1600. h. 9¾ in. (25.4 cm.). Museum of the American Indian, Heye Foundation, New York. The climax of the art of the Mississippi Stage of Eastern Woodlands culture appears in this small stone statue of a warrior about to scalp his prostrate enemy. Scalping was the form taken in North America by the head hunting tradition.

86, 87 (opposite). **Painted pottery vase from Colombia and another from Ecuador.** h. 20½ in. (52 cm.), 26½ in. (67 cm.). Both Museum für Völkerkunde, Munich. Similar designs on Andean textiles probably provided the models for these simplified geometric spirals.

88. **Polished black pottery vessel in the shape of a jaguar-toothed god's head from Peru.** Chavín culture, *c.* 300 AD h. 8¼ in. (21 cm.).

89. **Carved wooden stele with a human face from Peru.** h. 65¾ in. (167 cm.). Both Museum für Völkerkunde, Munich. The head motif in S. America took many forms, some highly evolved (88), others quite rudimentary (89). The sources of the Chavín style are still uncertain, but the expression on the ceramic heads suggest a possible relationship with Han-period China.

tive motifs from the art of the high cultures were often very widely diffused among primitive peoples whose social organisation and religious concepts remained almost completely untouched by outside influences. Tribal migrations and the fluctuations of the linguistic families within South America need much more study and we are still uncertain about the epoch when the original population arrived.

ASIA AND AMERICA

Exactly when and how large the contribution was that came to the mature American cultures across the Pacific from Asia is hard to tell. There are neither written nor oral histories that record it, and we can only go by conjectures based on common cultural features. These fall into two categories:

1 motifs of the hunter cultures—the animal style in rock paintings generally (the X-ray style in particular) and shamanist motifs

2 motifs associated with early food-producers, and features pointing to a relationship with the mature cultures of Asia—the latter include certain specialised motifs such as the scroll or meander motif. Early agriculturalist art and beliefs in America are exemplified by the skull and scalping motifs which originate in head-hunting, and the tiger-motif which has parallels in the archaic Chinese emblems seen on Shang and Chou bronzes.

Effective as these stimuli from the Old World must have

been, the geographical remoteness of America meant that contact can only have occurred in spasms, without a sustained cultural exchange taking place. Owing to their isolation, the American mature cultures remained much more closely linked to the sub-stratum of primitive cultures out of which they developed. Their accomplishments enhanced and intensified those of the preceding primitive cultures but are not divorced from them. Instead, they refined and polished what already existed until, as in Peru, it eventually died of rigidity or, as in Mexico, was lost in immoderate elaboration.

Boat-building and the navigation of rafts must have reached a fairly high level of accomplishment among peoples bordering on the Pacific as early as the Neolithic period. Researches into the settlement of the islands of Oceania prove that by the first half of the Han period (the last two centuries BC) people could have sailed from Asia to the eastern archipelagoes of Polynesia, and there is no reason why they could not have continued the voyage to America. The whole west coast of America was receptive to influences which were pouring out of Asia, either *via* the Bering Strait or across the Pacific, even during the first millennium BC. It is only curious that some very useful knowledge seems to have gone overboard on the way. The disappearance of the wheel—including the potter's wheel—is astonishing. It is hard to imagine how inventions like these could have been forgotten, even during a migration that lasted for several generations.

84, 85, 88

80, 81

Africa

In Africa, all the prehistoric cultural movements that we have traced across the continents of the world seem, at last, not only to converge but to co-exist without significantly influencing each other. There are masterpieces of the early hunting peoples' rock art in the central Sahara and in the Cape of Good Hope, there is also a homogeneous agriculturalist art throughout the Negro areas of West and Central Africa, and there are innumerable vestiges of the influences of the high cultures of the Mediterranean, both before and after the advent of Islam, in North Africa.

Africa is no more uniform in culture than it is in its geography. Africans are not one race of primitive 'blacks', nor is Africa, as is still too commonly thought, a continent without ancient history. The inhabitants stem from various races which may have their origin both locally and in Asia. Their cultural, ethnic and linguistic divisions are pronounced. Their past, though often obscure, is not a story of isolation. From the time of the earliest known hominids, living a million years ago in the Olduvai gorge, Africa has had an important place in human history. Ancient Egyptian and Greco-Roman influences linked the Sudan and the Niger lands with Mediterranean Europe. Indonesian influences linked Madagascar and East Africa with South-East Asia and so with the Chinese civilisation of the Shang period. Islam linked northern Africa as far as the Niger and the upper Nile with the Middle East and Spain.

Although the main types of prehistoric culture have survived in their pure form despite the long and thorough process of absorption of outside stimuli (hunter cultures untouched by agriculture are found among the Bushmen of the Kalahari desert, and the archaic farmer culture remained intact in their original state throughout the Negro area until the coming of the Europeans), there are a few areas where hybrid art styles developed out of the contact between cultures which was still further modified by contact with the high cultures of the Mediterranean across the Sahara.

What we normally term African or Negro art today is not spread throughout the length and breadth of the continent, but flourishes in one broad zone, inhabited by mainly agricultural peoples of basically related Bantu stock, and stretching from Guinea in the west to Katanga in the south-east. In other words, major African art is found exclusively in the river systems of the Niger and the Congo. East and south of this zone, from the Abyssinian highlands down to the European settlements of southern Africa, there lives a sober, stock-raising population which is hardly familiar with visual art in the true sense, though they are given to ornamenting their belongings and utensils—which are of functional and often elegant shape—with simple patterns.

The Negro population of Africa has, in fact, been migrating steadily southward in successive waves. The earliest dateable finds of agriculturalist African art are in eastern Nigeria and testify to the existence of well-devel-

90. **Prehistoric rock engravings of antelope and giraffes at Wadi Masauda, Fezzan,** drawn over with chalk. From the upper Nile valley to the Atlas mountains, the Sahara is rich in prehistoric rock art, with pictures of game that abounded in the pre-desert pasturelands.

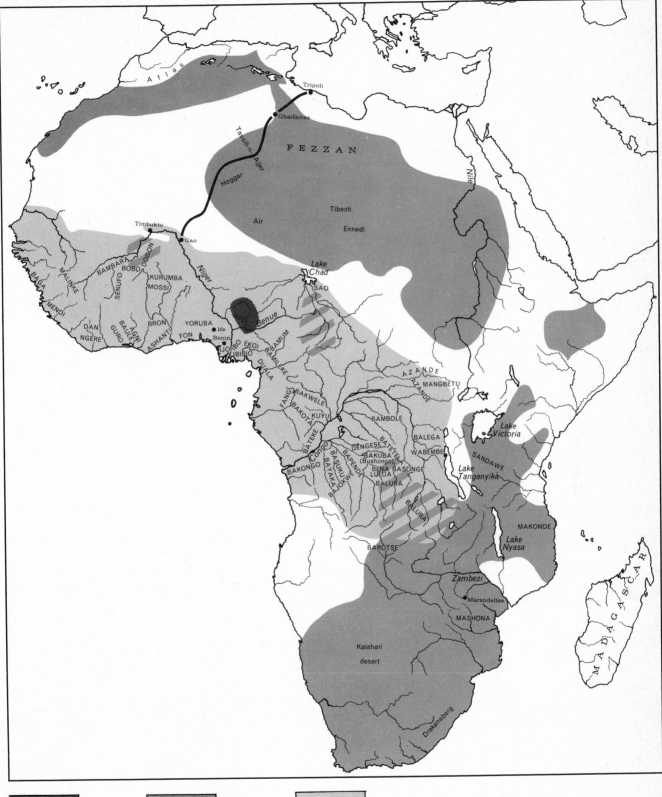

CHART J: AFRICA

Area of the Nok culture   Areas where rock art occurs   Main area of Negro sculpture

The 'chariot road'

91. **Dogon statue of an ancestral couple carved in wood from Mali.** h. 26¼ in. (66.5 cm.). Rietberg Museum, von der Heydt collection, Zürich. Like the famous, almost abstract Dogon masks, the figures display elongated architectural forms linked with native pre-Arab styles of N. Africa.

oped farming cultures with accomplished terracotta sculpture several centuries BC. This migration did not cease until less than a century ago when it clashed with the opposing movement of white settlers in the Cape, which on its side had been gaining momentum since the early seventeenth century. Survivors of the simple hunters and food-gatherers of much more ancient times are the pygmies of the Congo rain forest and the Bushmen of the Kalahari desert. The pygmies, who have been enclosed within the Negro area, produced no art, but the Bushmen, and their now extinct relatives the Hottentots, produced the vivacious rock paintings and engravings in pure hunter style for which they are famous.

The art of North Africa, being Islamic and thus of Middle Eastern origin, is not generally thought of as 'African', but we must remember that the elements of colour and form which the Arabs introduced in the seventh and eighth centuries AD blended easily with the ancient Berber art of the lands north and west of the Sahara. Islamic art has, however, radiated south of the Sahara, quite deeply into Negro Africa, where its acceptance has been far from complete. The abstract ornamental lines of the Islamic style do not easily accord with the Negro's very plastic and dynamic sense of form. It is noticeable that in the zone of contact between the two, sculpture often tends to become abstract and monumental, as in the masks of the Dogon and Bambara people in Mali, **90** whereas the Islamic use of colour in textiles finds its way *91* down to the coastal peoples of the Gulf of Guinea.

STONE AGE ART IN AFRICA

At a time when the Negro peoples had not yet spread far from an ancestral centre that probably lay around Lake Chad—the Sahara was a vast parkland watered by great rivers and teeming with game of every size. Throughout the Pleistocene Age, when the glaciers advanced and receded several times across Europe and northern Asia, the rainbelts seem to have made the Sahara a pleasant region for the hominids and Neanderthal men, whose flint tools have been found there in great quantities. A drier period in the early Old Stone Age then introduced a long moist period in which primitive hunters subsisted on the archaic species of elephant, hippopotamus, crocodile, giraffe, buffalo and many other wild animal that abounded there.

Rock pictures illustrate cultural movements of which *90* there is no other record. In the Atlas mountains of Algeria there are monumental engravings which are indubitable evidence of the southward spread from northern Spain of the Franco-Cantabrian hunter style. Curiously enough, this imposing and elegant style failed to spread to the south of Spain itself and, although confined there to the Basque provinces, leap-frogged to North Africa where it recurs so plentifully. It can then be traced, *via* East Africa, to the J most southerly part of the continent.

A most vivid record of the Neolithic period of human life **82,83**

86 in northern Africa is provided by the famous rock pictures in the desolate Tassili-n-Ajjer highlands in the central Sahara, roughly equidistant from the Mediterranean and the middle reaches of the Niger river. Known previously from some nineteenth-century travellers' accounts, these reproduced properly in 1959 by Henri Lhote, the French explorer and art historian.

Lhote's by now world-famous studies resulted in a provisional classification of the Sahara rock pictures, which have found general acceptance. For the fact is that 83 in the Tassili alone some twenty thousand separate figures have already been recorded—overlapping, superimposed or adjacent, and clearly belonging to a long sequence of succeeding epochs of uncertain duration.

The earliest group of pictures is likely to be of those of human figures with round, almost featureless heads shaped like suet puddings, which is dated to the beginning of the Neolithic age, about 8000 BC. Occasionally the heads are adorned with what look like horns or feathers, and the resemblance to men in space helmets with their antennae has caused these figures to be dubbed the 'Martians'. Painted usually in flat monochrome, the bulbous figures represent men hunting with bows and arrows and women whose hands seem to be raised in supplication. An intense religious feeling runs through many of these enigmatic pictures of human beings, while the paintings and polished-outline engravings of the animals mentioned above have the characteristic hunter style naturalism. The round-headed pictures often share the rock face with larger paintings and engravings of a second type which are the work of a different people, though they, too, obviously depended on hunting the same wild ox, *bubalus antiquus*, which is depicted in both styles. It is not known whether the two populations co-existed during the period from about 8000 to 6000 BC, nor where either of them came from, nor whether one preceded the other. It seems, however, from the scarifications indicated on the round-headed 83 figures (which resemble those raised on their skin by many West Africans today) and from obvious masks of Negro type associated with some of the figures, that this was a Negroid people who may have migrated northward from Lake Chad, while the 'Europoid' features of the larger figures of the other type suggest an origin either in the Mediterranean or in the Middle East.

The next group of pictures begins to appear about the fifth millennium BC and coincides with the arrival of several waves of numerous herdsmen who moved in from the east, possibly from the upper Nile. The rock pictures consist of 82 cattle in vast numbers and show that the earlier waves brought sheep and goats (of the same breed as are still kept by the Tuareg nomads in the Sahara today), followed later by great herds of oxen. Carbon-14 analysis of ash from their camping sites has given dates of 3500 to 2500 BC, but the pastoralist style probably spanned a period of several thousand years. The herdsmen seem to have been a copper-skinned 'Nilotic' people similar to the Ethiopians,

92. **Bangwa house-post carved in wood from Cameroon.** h. 9 ft. 9¼ in. (298 cm.). Museum für Völkerkunde, Munich. An ancient motif of the farmer cultures of S.-E. Asia in full use in equatorial Africa—a genealogical 'tree' consisting of squatting ancestor figures. The Bangwa are a sub-group of the Bamileke (see Chart J).

93. **Bangwa standing ancestor figure.** h. 36¼ in. (92 cm.). Museum für Völkerkunde, Munich. This figure is typical of the bent-knees motif in African sculpture. The Bangwa style can be seen here and in figure 92.

but they may have absorbed the earlier inhabitants, as there continue to be scenes of hunting and fishing alongside the evidence of more settled life in villages and of semi-nomadic cattle-raising. At this time the Sahara was still a land of plenty, but the study of fossilised pollen reveals that by about 2000 BC the great dessication of North Africa was on the way.

86,87

The moist and tropical conditions known to the Neolithic hunters who produced the earliest rock art had been replaced by the Mediterranean climate and vegetation of the pastoralist period, in which *bubalus antiquus* had become extinct, the hippopotamus and rhinoceros disappeared, while the elephant retreated to a few grassy regions to survive until the time of the Carthaginians. (Hannibal's war-elephants must have been caught and trained on the southern fringes of modern Tunisia and Algeria). By the end of the pastoralist period, conditions in the Sahara approximated to the savannah of the upper Niger and the southern Sudan today, but aridity began to increase rapidly from now on. Other changes were also in the offing. This was the moment in history when the domestication of the horse became known in the Middle East. By 1200 BC, warlike peoples on the Mediterranean coast of Africa had equipped themselves with chariots and set out on raids into the interior. At once a new style of rock picture makes its appearance on the walls of the Tassili rock shelters, influenced by Egyptian models of the Eighteenth Dynasty (1557–1304 BC) and depicting chariot-borne warriors.

The invading chariot-people and the local herdsmen have both left us a pictorial record of this warfare. There are many scenes of battle and we see the bows and arrows of the natives being used against the javelins, shields and war-chariots of the conquerors. For the chariot-people clearly won. Henceforward there are no more pictures in the pastoralist style. By means of the rock pictures, Henri Lhote has succeeded in tracing the 'chariot road' of the J

(Continued on page 161)

82 (opposite). **Cattle.** 'Bovidian' period, *c.* 5000–1200 BC. Polychrome painting on rock. l. 46 in. (3 m.). Jabbaren rock shelter, Tassili-n-Ajjer, Algeria. The frontiers of African art are being pushed further and further back in time. We now know that rock pictures in what was then the fertile, well watered Sahara are as old, at least, as the cave art of eastern Spain (the 'Spanish Levant' or 'Second Hunter Style', *c.* 6000–2000 BC). This herd of hastening cattle, drawn in several solid colours with absolute assurance, is among the spectacular finds made since 1957—by Henri Lhote and others in the central Sahara. The artists were nomadic herdsmen (hence the term, 'Bovidian' period) who came from the east. Their style drew its inspiration from the hunter style of the Spanish Levant and this was transmitted through the whole length of Africa to primitive hunting peoples in the Cape. The Bushmen of the Kalahari desert kept this rock picture style alive until the middle of the 19th century.

83 (opposite). **The 'White Lady' of Aouanrhet.** 'Bovidian' period, *c.* 5000–1200 BC. Copy of rock painting. h. (of figure) 43¼ in. (110 cm.). Tassili-n-Ajjer, Algeria. This vigorous and rhythmic painting of a dancing priestess or goddess, superimposed on lively groups of hunting or fighting figures, illustrates the early farming peoples' interest in depicting the human figure, especially in motion. The link between this anthropomorphic naturalism and fertility beliefs shows in the stylised wheat-field floating over her horned headdress. In ritual dancing in West Africa today the same shivering, rippling movement of the fringes on her arms and hips can be observed. Note the realistic scarification on the skin and the magic objects in the hands, as well as the other version of the same subject lower down.

84 (above right). **Human hand and three figures.** Prehistoric. Copy of rock painting. 9½ in. (24 cm.). Wadi Sera, Libya.

85 (below right). **Human hand with dots.** Date unknown. Copy of rock painting. h. 10 in. (26 cm.). Domboshawa region, Rhodesia. The motif of outlined hands shows the continuity of hunter-culture rock art as it spread from the caves of western Europe (plate 2) across northern Africa (plate 84) to southern Africa (plate 85). Later figures of dancers and of a hunter have been painted on top of the two African hands.

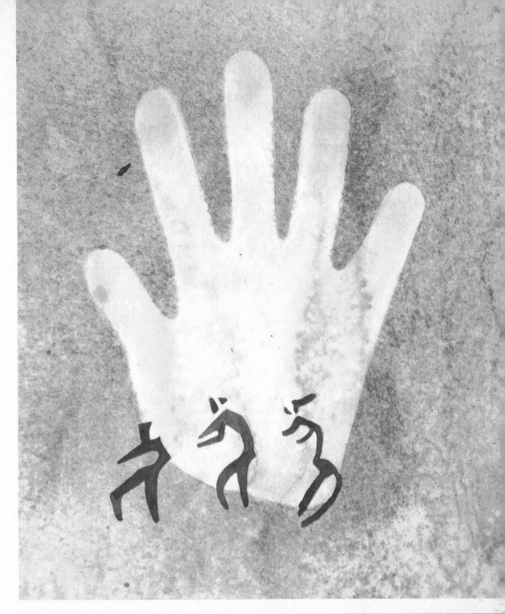

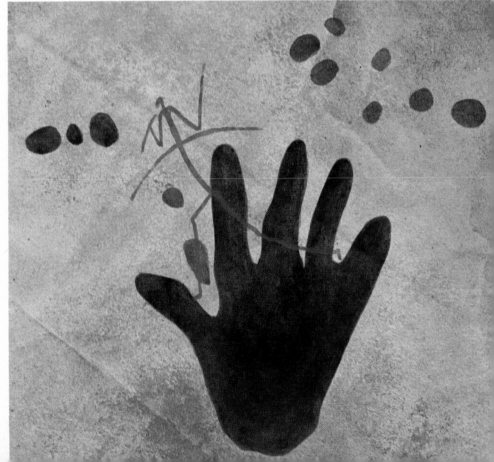

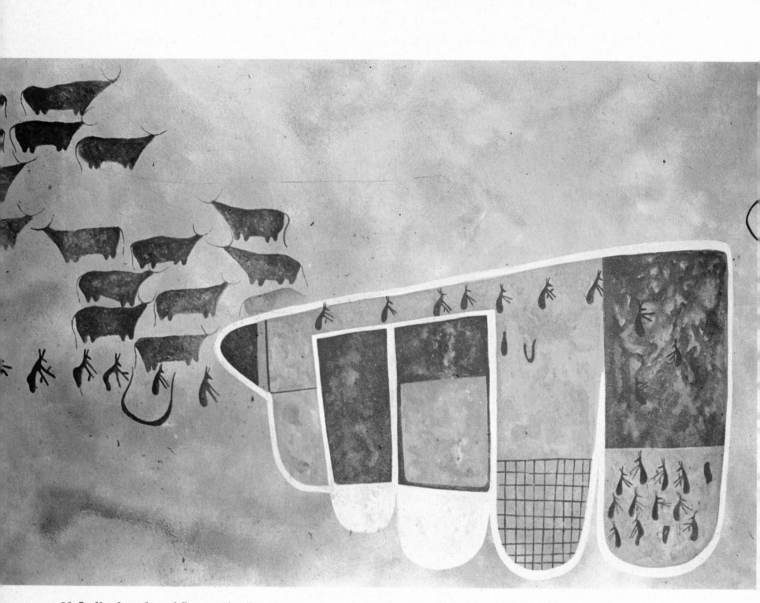

86. **Stylised cattle and figures** (detail).
'Bovidian' period, *c.* 5000–1200 BC. Copy
of a rock painting. l. 6 ft. 10½ in. (210 cm.).
Ti-n-Tazarift rock shelter, Tassili-n-Ajjer,
Algeria. A more stylised painting of the
herdsman period (plates 82, 83). The
shapes in the centre and right may
represent huts or cattle-pens. The meaning
of the animal-headed figures is still
uncertain.

87 (opposite, left). **Battle of archers**
(detail). Copy of rock painting.
Khargur-Talch, Libya. Action pulses
through this picture of a fierce battle for,
apparently, possession of a bull. A barrage
of arrows flies from either side. The
bottom figure on the right is wearing
an animal mask. The movement of the
figures recalls the Spanish Levant rock
pictures.

88 (opposite, right). **Rain ceremony,**
also called the 'Tree of Life'. Date
unknown. Copy of rock painting. h. 7 ft.
(213 cm.). Waltondale Farm,
Marandellas, Rhodesia. The rain
ceremony is the people's attempt at
communion with the spirits of the sky.
East African Wahungwe myths explain
the scene as follows: a virgin of the royal
house is being buried alive at the foot of a
tree; when its top reaches the sky, a snake
crawls out of the branches and sends the
people the rain which is seen spouting
over the girl's body. A goddess is visible
in the sky above the snake.

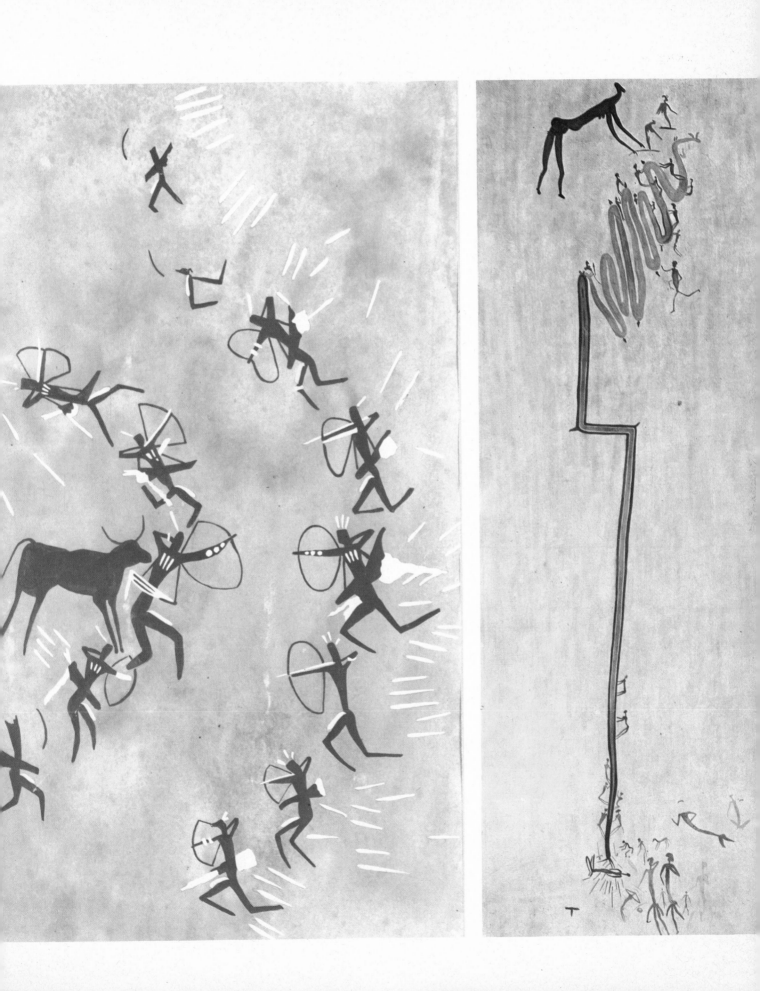

89 (below). **Rhinoceros hunt.** Date
unknown. Copy of rock painting.
l. *c.* 31½ in. (80 cm.). Naukluft, S.-W.
Africa.

92 (on pages 152–3). **Large composite
painting.** Date unknown. Copy of rock
painting. l. *c.* 23½ ft. (7.2 m.). Mtoko
Cave, Rhodesia. Even in southern Africa
the hunter style remained constant. Like
the battle in plate 87, this rhinoceros hunt
recalls the Spanish Levant rock pictures,
while the great composite scene in
plate 92 shows a flourishing tradition
of rock art. The Mtoko painting

is the work of many artists, probably of
many generations, superimposed. Its
details are full of interest. One can pick
out elegantly drawn horses, zebras,
quaggas, gnus, elands and other
antelopes, baboons and, of course,
numerous active human figures, some
wearing masks. The large scale elephant
at the top is evidently one of the earliest
paintings on the site. The zigzag double
line across the middle may be a rain-snake
(see plate 88). The four curious shapes at
the bottom left could represent mountains
or a village.

90 (right). **Bambara cloth from Mali, W. Africa.** (detail). 19th century. Printed cotton. l. (of whole) 51¼ in. (130 cm.). Rietberg Museum, Zürich. The pattern seen in this detail is repeated all along the material. It is formed of an abstraction from a row of squatting ancestor figures one above the other—the familiar genealogical motif from S.-E. Asia. The severe geometrical style is due to the influence of Islam south of the Sahara.

91 (below). **Carved prow from Douala, Cameroon.** Late 19th century. Painted wood. h. 31½ in. (80 cm.). Museum für Völkerkunde, Munich. This delightful extravaganza of mythological creatures and uniformed Europeans shows a confident sense of formal construction. Such vitality is typical of African Negro art, but the strong resemblance between boats prows in Melanesia and Cameroon is also well known. It is a classic clue to the spread of ancient motifs round the world.

93 (opposite). **Kurumba dance head-dress in the form of an antelope's head from Aribinda,** Upper Volta, W. Africa. 20th century. Painted wood. h. 43 in. (109 cm.). Museum für Völkerkunde, Munich.

94. **Senufo figure of a standing bird, Ivory Coast,** W. Africa. 20th century. Painted wood. h. 4 ft. 7½ in. (141 cm.). Museum für Völkerkunde, Munich.

The Kurumba and Senufo peoples are neighbours who are separated by the border between two African republics. The art of the middle Niger region, lying between the Sahara and the coastal forests, has a dry elegance which is seen in both of these pieces. The forms of hunter art were continued by the agricultural tribes (including the Dogon, Bambara, Mossi and others) but the anti-pictorial influence of Islam on their art has imparted a certain rigidity to surface decoration. The antelope crests (plate 93) are bound to the heads of dancers in mourning and sowing rituals. The bird image (plate 94) has genealogical figures on the back, and probably played a part in the ancestor cult. The pattern and colouring on the formal, rectangular wings recall Melanesian art.

95 (opposite, above left). **Head probably of an early Oni of Ife,** from Ife, Nigeria. 13th–14th centuries. Bronze. h. 14¼ in. (36 cm.).

96 (opposite, above right). **Pendant mask from Benin,** Nigeria. Probably 16th century. Ivory. h. 7½ in. (19 cm.).

97 (opposite, below left). **Head of a queen mother (iyoba) from Benin,** Nigeria. Probably 16th century. Bronze. h. 15½ in. (39 cm.). 95, 96, 97 from the British Museum, London.

98 (opposite, below right). **Poro secret society mask of the Dan tribe,** Liberia. Date unknown. Wood. h. 9½ in. (24 cm.). Museum für Völkerkunde, Munich. The masks and heads of West Africa are masterpieces of Negro art and display enormous imaginative variety. The contrast which the world-famous portrait sculpture of Ife and Benin (95, 97) makes to formal and symbolic masks (98) may be due to Mediterranean influences.

99. **Hunter carrying an antelope.** From Benin, Nigeria. Probably late 19th century. Bronze. h. 14½ in. (37 cm.). British Museum, London. The bronzes of Ife and Benin (plates 95, 97) are ranked among the great achievements of world art. Benin learned bronze casting from Ife about 1280 and developed a robust, though rather heavy, expressionist style of its own with, as here, a tendency to good-humoured caricature.

158

100 (below left). **Bena Lulua female figure from S.-E. Congo.** 19th century. Painted wood. h. 11 in. (28 cm.). Museum für Völkerkunde, Munich. Sculpture in the Congo faithfully follows tribal tradition, but every local variation adds to the luxuriance of forms. This female

ancestor figure is shown with an exaggerated navel and in the bent-knees stance characteristic of Oceanic art.

101 (below right). **Bakuba fabric** (called 'Kasai velvet') from Kasai, Congo (detail). 19th century. Raffia. h. (of

whole) 26 in. (71 cm.). Museum für Völkerkunde, Munich. The geometric treatment of the spiral on this pleasantly toned hanging from the western Congo encloses a motif comparable with the Peruvian 'jaguar's eye' textile (plate 79).

102. **Makonde monkey mask from south-east Tanzania.** 20th century. Wood. h. 8¼ in. (21 cm.). Museum für Völkerkunde, Munich. East Africa (like southern Africa below the Zambezi) belongs to a zone where the hunter and herdsman styles prevailed, with little or no sculpture in the farmer style. Masks like this clown's one from near the sea coast close to the Mozambique border are very unusual. The blobs of clay may represent hair on the monkey's face.

94. Bakundu wooden carving of ten human figures from western Cameroon. h. 17¼ in. (44 cm.). Museum für Völkerkunde, Munich. The meaning and use of this curious piece is not known, but it is interestingly composed and may represent a line of ancestors arranged in an unusual way.

period known as 'Wiltonian'. Cooke does not think it likely that paintings could have survived for longer than six thousand years in the open air. Style I consists of animals in motion and stylised human figures.

Style II is not more than two thousand years old and consists of animal silhouettes drawn in outline and filled in with pigment. The stylised human figures are painted without any preliminary sketch.

The later *Styles III, IV* and *V* become progressively livelier in the depiction of animals and humans and come to an end with the arrival of the Europeans.

The correlation of rock art, which extends down Africa from north to south by way of the lands east of the great lakes, with Negro art, which occupies the west and centre, has never yet been undertaken by scholars. Yet we have seen that Bushman art in the Bantu Style (to use Walton's classification) appears to have reached a peak of virtuosity precisely when the Bantu (or Negro) peoples were dispossessing them of their ancestral hunting grounds. Likewise, along the northern fringe of Negro art in West Africa, among the Dogon on the Niger, in Mali, abstract rock pictures are found, though these resemble masks more than animals, while there are also some scattered examples of abstract rock pictures on the southern fringe of Negro art, in northern Angola. It may be that apart from these slight contacts, no connection at all exists between the two. From separate origins they may have developed and existed side by side without interaction.

NEGRO ART

African Negro art proper, and especially sculpture, is extremely uniform and is confined to the areas in which the population is engaged in settled agriculture. It has developed exclusively from the cults of ancestor-worship. The symbols of plant and of seed, of the quickening of life out of death, have been the determining factors in the cosmology of these peasant peoples, and their whole art is rooted in them. Their images represent ancestors, their masks deputise for the spirits of deceased forebears who speak through them to the present generation, and in their decorative art both of these motifs are employed in profusion. This cosmology and this artistic style have strong affinities with those of South-East Asia. It is reasonable to suppose that these were introduced into Africa, along with the Neolithic culture, which came by sea *via* Madagascar from Indonesia.

Little that is definite can yet be said about the antiquity of Negro art. The sculpture is mostly in wood, as it has probably always been, with the result that it perishes easily. The first finds pointing to a great age for Negro art were made by Bernard Fagg in 1943, north of the Benue river in eastern Nigeria. There, near a village called Nok, he uncovered terracotta heads and figurines, skilfully executed in a style of great perfection, which are now well-known as the oldest and among the most attractive African works of art. Their sophisticated naturalism can be traced

95. **Carved and painted wooden snake from Yaoundé,**
Cameroon. l. 55¼ in. (140 cm.). Museum für Völkerkunde,
Munich. The painted pattern on this naturalistically carved
snake is a further example of the similarity that has been noted
between the art of Cameroon and of Melanesia (see plate 91,
figure 92). Snake figures of this kind are also made by the Baga
of Guinea.

without much difficulty to Mediterranean influence from
across the Sahara, perhaps by means of the 'chariot road'.
According to Carbon-14 dating, the Nok culture flourished
over a wide area in the Benue valley between 900 BC and
200 AD, but was probably concentrated in the last four or
five centuries BC. The beginning of this style coincided with
the introduction of iron from the east or north.

If the roundly-modelled naturalism of the Nok culture
heads has affinities with Mediterranean art (whether
ancient Egyptian or Hellenistic), other waves of outside
influence, which can be verified historically, have left
hardly a few traces on Negro art. They do, however,
provide a key to dating.

After masks, Negro sculpture consists almost entirely of
ancestor images. These are human figures with, by and
large, a high degree of uniformity of style, wherever they
come from. Almost invariably they stand with slight flexion
of the legs. Here we find again the motif which, as we saw
on page 133, is equally distinctive of 'Circumpacific'
art, having evolved from the squatting ancestor figure of
the primitive farmers in South-East Asia. Presumably it
was brought to East Africa by way of Madagascar, an
island which was colonised and populated from across the
Indian Ocean. (The people of Madagascar speak an
Austronesian language, and are related to the Neolithic
sea-faring immigrants from South-East Asia who spread
into Indonesia and Oceania). The Sakalava tribe in

Madagascar have sculpture which is as much Indonesian
in style as it is African.

Most people are aware of the impressive bronzes from
Benin on the west coast of Africa, but fine though these are,
they do not represent the highest achievement of African
sculptors and bronze-founders in this style. The Benin
work goes back to the school of Ife, also in western Nigeria,
and it was from here that the rulers of Benin obtained the
artists who founded their own somewhat stiffer school of
bronze sculpture. The elegant bronze and ivory figures
from Ife, on the other hand, are undoubtedly masterpieces
of the front rank. From about the ninth century AD, Ife
was the religious and cultural centre of the Yoruba tribe,
and the great heads and figures in the Ife style as we know
it can be assigned, from associated finds, to the thirteenth
century. But Ife in its turn was dependent on the Nok style
of eastern Nigeria, one and a half millennia earlier. The
territory of the energetic and alert Yoruba seems to have
acted—though we lack any written records of this—as a
sort of cultural catchment-area for most of the ancient
Egyptian, Classical and Early Christian-Byzantine stimuli
that came into Negro Africa from the north. It radiated a
powerful artistic influence far and wide.

Excavations in the sites of the Nok Culture in Nigeria
have brought to light some most exciting finds which were
first published by William Fagg in 1951. These are fragments of a terracotta group of nude figures in motion. Their

supple modelling is unmistakably Hellenistic in feeling, and scholars are now being obliged to revise accepted ideas about the relationship of African cultures with those outside. The old view that there were no external stimuli seems to have been refuted, and contacts with the Mediterranean world must have thrived on a scale we could not hitherto suspect.

When the Benin kingdom was overthrown by a British punitive expedition in 1897, well over two thousand bronze works quickly became known in Europe. Only then did the world realise that West Africa boasted a bronze art of such high distinction that collectors rushed to acquire the looted pieces. For a time it was debated whether Benin work ought to be ascribed to foreign—in this context, Portuguese—influence. The Portuguese had traded with Benin in the sixteenth and seventeenth centuries, and they were often portrayed in detail on the bronze plaques which were made for the Benin kings.

The recent Nigerian finds now answer this question of outside influence rather differently: the bronzes of the Benin kingdom, dating from the period between the fifteenth and seventeenth centuries, are an African elaboration of influences derived from the high cultures of European Classical antiquity and transmitted through the Yoruba tribe. Many centuries before the Portuguese merchants sailed into the Gulf of Guinea, Mediterranean stimuli had had their effect there. Stylistic comparison with West African bronzes may even point, in Annemarie Schweger-Hefel's opinion, to the Etruscans as a source. Europe and Africa were linked at a very ancient date, and although the existence of their ties was forgotten for many centuries, the more we find out about Africa's past, the more clearly they reappear.

AFRICA AND EUROPE

From the Mesolithic period up to the late Islamic conquests in the Mediterranean lands there was a constant cultural traffic between Europe and Africa. Ties between the two continents were at this time so close that even two style groups which differed greatly from one another—the Franco-Cantabrian monumental animal style and the Second Hunter style of the Spanish Levant with human figures—are found co-existing in Africa as in Europe.

Throughout their existence, the ancient Mediterranean high cultures made themselves felt in North Africa, and radiated from the coastal area across the Sahara. The distant echo of the Mediterranean world was caught by Frobenius when, in northern Togo in 1909, he recorded the epic poem *Gassire's Lute*. This epic conjures up the picture of a heroic-age feudal culture that had come from the sea in the north, making a halt at several intermediate points, and finally settling in the Sudan to the west of Timbuktu. The epic mentions an aristocratic people called the *Fasa*, which calls to mind the Greek name for the Fezzan: *Phazania*. The name of the tribe to whom the singer belonged was Djerma, which is suggestive of the ancient

96. **Bakota 'mbulu ngulu' figure in beaten sheet copper from Gaboon.** h. 22 in. (56 cm.). Museum für Völkerkunde, Munich. These metal-covered Bakota heads, now prized by collectors, are evil-averting ancestor figures placed on top of boxes or baskets in which a chief's skull is preserved. The expression is reminiscent of the grave power of some Romanesque sculpture in Europe.

Garama, the former capital of Fezzan, and the Garamantes tribe, known to Classical writers. About 400 BC, Herodotus, who had a thorough knowledge of the North African coastlands, described the Garamantes as industrious farmers, who raised livestock and rode into battle in chariots drawn by four horses. In the year 19 BC the Romans conquered the oasis of Phazania, defeated the Garamantes and advanced to the oasis to Ghadames. At the beginning of the second century AD, the Roman general, Julius Maternus, penetrated far south to a land called Aghisymba—which we can take to be the oasis of Agades on the central Saharan plateau of Aïr, 700 miles south of Tassili. With this advance the Romans thus reached areas where no European was again to set foot until the travels of the German scholar, Heinrich Barth, in the eighteen-fifties. The feudal culture which Herodotus reported near the shores of the Mediterranean was probably displaced southward under Roman pressure, and reminiscences of it have survived, in this one epic at least, in the western Sudan up to modern times.

At the end of the Classical period and in the early centuries of the Christian empire, North Africa had for a time a very attractive place within the universal Mediterranean culture. The Church flourished from Carthage to Alexandria, producing great saints and disturbing heresies. Monasticism was born in the Egyptian desert, and both Tertullian and Saint Augustine were North Africans. Mauretania and Numidia were still bastions of the Byzantine empire at a time when the Western Roman empire was already occupied by the Goths. A number of Oriental motifs, especially in their Syrian and Coptic versions remain detectable in North Africa and the Sudan as a heritage of Byzantine art even today. In Abyssinia, an outlier of Monophysite Syrian Christianity has survived to the present day in union with the Coptic Church of Egypt, an enclave separated from the rest of the Christian world by the tidal wave of Islam.

During the eighth century AD the incursions of Islam from Asia to the Atlantic coasts of Morocco and Spain introduced a new element into the Eurafrican culture of the Mediterranean, and for eight hundred years sealed Europe off from Africa. In the area under their sway, however, the Arabs inherited the legacy of Classical antiquity and diffused Mediterranean skills and craftsmanship in Africa. They also continued, in their eclectic way, the classical learning and scholarship which had flourished on North African soil. The geographical works of Ptolemy, information about Africa collected during the second century AD, remained unknown in Europe until the fifteenth century, but were translated into Arabic as early as the ninth century. The Arabs were well versed in geography, and their knowledge was extended by the pilgrimages which the faithful were encouraged to make to Mècca. These involved protracted journey throughout the whole area under Muslim rule, and the exploration of Africa was to a large extent the work of early Islamic travellers. Edrisi (1099–1186), a member of a princely

97. **Baluba figure of a woman carved in wood from Urua,** Congo. h. 19 in. (48 cm.). Museum für Völkerkunde, Munich. The Baluba dominate a large group of peoples in the S.-E. Congo and the influence of their style reaches Zambia, Malawi and Rhodesia. The Makonde style (plate 102) is related to it. This figure is a masterpiece of Baluba sculpture (see figures 98, 99, 100). The woman's hair-style and the scarifications on her belly are typical of personal adornment in this area.

98–99. **Two Baluba female ancestor figures in carved wood with fibre skirts from Urua,** Congo. h. 13 in., 14½ in. (33 cm., 37 cm.). Museum für Völkerkunde, Munich. The fame of Baluba sculpture rests on the Baluba artists' sense of plastic values and preference for flowing, graceful forms (see figures 97, 100). Both of these ancestor figures display the motif of flexion of the legs.

family from Moorish Spain, journeyed from his native town of Ceuta through Morocco to the interior of Africa, and his map of the world, compiled for Roger II of Sicily, formed the basis for all later maps of Africa until the eighteenth century.

In north-western Africa, the Berber element in Islam comes out strongly. The famous medieval Moslem traveller, Ibn Batuta (Abu Abdullah Mahommed, 1304–1378) was a Berber from Tangier. He spent nearly thirty years travelling in Asia, Africa, and parts of Europe, and was the first to describe the extensive trading city of Timbuktu on the Niger. Leo Africanus, the author of the *Description of Africa*, published at the behest of Pope Leo X in 1526, was another Berber traveller, whose real name was Al Hassan Ibn Mohammed al Wezaz (1492–1526). Born in Granada, he visited the Saharan and Sudanese regions of Africa, including Timbuktu, in 1513–1515. So intense was the penetration of North Africa by Islam that for many centuries Europeans used the terms 'Moor' and 'Barbary' as synonyms for 'African'—particularly so long as little was known about Negro Africa proper. This confusion is vividly brought out in Shakespeare's *Othello*, where the author is obviously uncertain whether the 'Moor' of Venice is a Negro or a Moslem North African. Negro Africa was only discovered by the Portuguese when from 1416 onwards, in the course of their efforts to find a sea-route to India around Africa, Portuguese ships visited West Africa every year. They reached the coast of Guinea around the middle of the fifteenth century and in the following century set up trading posts in Benin. These Portuguese colonies forged

the first modern links between Europe and Africa, and the impact of Portuguese colonisation at that time can be gauged from the art of the Bakongo on the lower Congo and in the subjects illustrated, almost affectionately, in the bronzes of Benin.

The carving up of Africa among the European colonial powers began in the eighteenth century and was brought to a conclusion at the end of the nineteenth century. The political map of the modern African states reflects this arbitrary partitioning of the continent during the age of imperialism. The structure of African culture broke down when the political arrangements of the nineteenth century were made without regards for the pattern of existing African development. Only in the present day do we see the old centres gradually resuming their former role as focal points of advancement. The dialogue between modern Europe and Africa reaches its climax in the twentieth century.

If we survey the chief contributions made by Europeans to the study of the African cultures, we shall readily agree that, while the German anthropologist Leo Frobenius was the first European scholar to emphasise repeatedly that Africa was not inhabited by 'savages' but had produced many cultures with an intrinsic value of their own, most of the work has been done by French scholars, both on the Islamic lands and on Negro culture proper. A mass of literary and artistic publications in French or by Frenchmen demonstrates this. The French began to explore Islamic Africa at the close of the nineteenth century. There was the Marquis de Castries, who began to work on the cartography of Morocco in 1881 and went on to compile a history of that country in sixteen volumes. He was a friend of Lyautey, the French administrator of Morocco, and of Charles de Foucauld. The latter travelled in eastern Morocco and spent fifteen years of his life as a hermit in the Hoggar, among the Tuareg tribes. Foucauld's Christian mysticism was greatly influenced by Islam, and his ascetic Order of the White Fathers owes some of its characteristic features to the example of the Moslem *marabouts* or holy men. De Foucauld, with his almost medieval religious zeal, was an outstanding linguist. He had perfect command of Arabic and compiled a Tuareg grammar and dictionary.

French men and women of letters of the Romantic movement helped to promote an understanding of Africa in Europe during the nineteenth century. One need think only of the writings of Isabella Eberhardt, Merimée, Nerval and Flaubert. In our own century, there is the influence of the diaries of André Gide. In Delacroix's 'Women of Algiers' or Henri Rousseau's 'The Sleeping Gypsy' one senses a deep inner understanding for the singular character of North African Islamic culture. The interest taken by the French in North Africa was not merely a matter of geographical proximity and colonial expansion. They revive, albeit unconsciously, a very ancient cultural relationship.

The dialogue between European artists and true Negro art in West Africa is hardly fifty years old. It began like-wise in France, and has indeed been carried on almost exclusively by the French. European artists in general have been attracted by the bizarre character of Negro art. They emulate it and adapt it, without, however, penetrating to the heart of its essential qualities. The only exception perhaps is Picasso, who, at the outset of his cubist phase, around 1907, undoubtedly derived decisive stimuli from African art, into the nature of which he has probed deeply and instinctively. He is the one artist who has succeeded in forging a synthesis of what is European and what is African in art.

AFRICAN ART TODAY

At the present time, African art has two important centres: the coast of West Africa, and the area of the river Congo. These two regions are related. The Baluba of northern Katanga, in particular, have adopted an unusually large number of elements from Yoruba art. The Pangwe (or Fang), who live to the north of the Ogowe river in Gaboon, have transplanted artistic forms into this area from the Islamised northern Sudan, as can clearly be seen in the abstraction of their masks.

We should not assume that things have always been as they are today. Less than a hundred years ago, some African tribes were still moving from one region to another and introducing their art with them. Migrations can still be observed taking place on a smaller scale today, and it must be assumed that this also occurred in earlier times. The African ability to digest stimuli from outside and to sustain

100. **Baluba ancestor figure carved in wood from Urua,** Congo. h. 19 in. (48 cm.). Museum für Völkerkunde, Munich. An aristocratic reserve is expressed by the features on Baluba heads—this is the art of an African empire. The treatment of the flexed legs is close to that of the Hawaiian statue in figure 77.

101 (left). **Nok culture head in terracotta.** 2nd–1st century BC. Jos Museum, Nigeria.

102 (opposite). **Wrought iron pole top in the form of an armed horseman from Nigeria.** h. of figure, 22½ in. (57 cm.). Museum für Völkerkunde, Munich. The terracotta heads of the early Iron Age Nok culture in Nigeria, with their roundly modelled naturalistic forms, have been known only for the past 25 years. Their discovery by the British archaeologist Bernard Fagg completely revolutionised our view of African Negro art. Ancient Egyptian or Hellenistic stimuli across the Sahara (Chart J) would account for a style differing radically from most other African Negro sculpture, in which affinities with the art of the early farmer cultures of S.-E. Asia are stronger. The later masterpieces of Ife and Benin (plates 95, 96, 97) probably stem from a Nok tradition. Iron was introduced during the Nok period and Nigerian artists are still noted for the bold and amusing forms of their wrought iron work (figure 102).

their effect over a lengthy period of time gave the first European observers the false impression that the people of this continent were hopelessly static in their culture. All the high cultures from outside Africa which penetrated the continent—in particular Negro Africa in the narrow sense—took from it more than they gave. The African is accustomed to oppression and dispossession at the hands of the advanced cultures. Denigrated as a savage, the African enters the stage of world history in Africa and America as an exploited slave, never as a conqueror. The Negro race has probably been exploited more and longer than any other, yet despite all that he has suffered the Negro has never lost his spiritual poise. The Negro's marked capacity for absorption and conservation is expressed in all the African culture and he retains this power even when uprooted from his soil and transplanted to another continent. The American Negro possesses an extraordinary strength of artistic creativity, imbuing utterly alien motifs with his singular quality. For example, the American Negro has created a new style of music, which now finds world-wide acceptance, both in secular jazz and in religious songs.

The Negro has a kind of sturdiness which allows him to take over alien cultural elements, however foreign they may be to his own nature, and mould them into a homogeneous form that suits his own temperament. Influences so overwhelming that he cannot escape from them, such as European Christianity, he works on for as long as may be necessary until they conform to his own feelings. African Christianity, with its innumerable sects, is a far cry from the white missionary's model, and a good deal more intense. Even Islamic art, which lends itself so extremely well to diffusion among foreign nations, has made only slow headway among the Negroes, and elements from it have been transformed by them out of recognition.

The Negro has shown considerable aptitude for statecraft, but seems to be best in his element in a small community, to the life of which he can impart a natural equilibrium and dignity. So long as he can live undisturbed, he continually tends to form communities. In the Guianas, in South America, settlements were founded by escaped slaves in which the ancestral way of life has been revived. The Negro does not relapse into primeval savagery, but even in foreign areas recovers his natural poise. In altered conditions he reconstructs the cultural and political environment that suits him best.

The danger that threatens Africa today is the uprooting of its agricultural population as a result of industrial development. Large areas have been depopulated by the needs for cheap labour in the mines and factories of the Congo, the Copper Belt and South Africa. The cattle lands are threatened with galloping soil erosion and the cover that remains in the limited native pastures is soon dislodged and blown away by the wind. One can only hope that the Negroes' natural staying power will not fail them in their present adversity.

The relationship between Europe and Africa is now political rather than cultural. In the previous century it was economic, but strongly tinged with missionary considerations. The Negro is capable of a tremendous intensity of religious belief. Only Islam, which actually puts into practice the principles of racial equality that must be implicit in religion, did and still does enjoy to any substantial degree the faith and fervour of the African, which in turn has often served in setting up and defending extensive Moslem states on the African continent. Opposed to Islam is Christianity, which for four hundred years has failed to put the ideal of human equality into practice, or to allow Africans to make their own contribution to the shaping of the world in which they live.

At the beginning of the Christian era there were of course no racial barriers. There were Christian Africans and African saints. The disastrous idea of racial barriers, of judging men by the colour of their skin, probably developed at the time of the Islamic conquest, when Christianity was in retreat. The fact that the religion found itself limited to Europe led to a narrowing of the Christian outlook, to the erroneous idea that only white men were Christians and created as true human beings. The infidels were not only incompletely human, they also had differently coloured skins. This calamitous prejudice, which has by no means been fully overcome in our own times, reduced relations between Europe and Africa to a barren paralysis until recent times.

What can art tell us about the nature of the African? In the first place we must note the intensity of his art and its limitation to very few themes—the absence of any wide range of variants. Art is spirit, and the further that development leads toward rationalism, the more man exhausts his spirit, and the poorer he becomes in artistic expression. This is obviously the problem of our age: the problem that faces Western man, who has driven the process of rationalisation that men are capable of to such a pitch that art has almost expired, or, at least, is generally regarded as threatened, and its future existence as problematical. Contrast with this the unexhausted spirit of the Negro, which perhaps cannot be exhausted since he is incapable of rationalisation. What seems to us to be his naivety, is simply vitality: vital energy that has taken a different course from ours, and is directed only toward expression of his inner self, and not toward the rationalising of existence. Modern Christian sculpture from Africa, shown in the exhibition in Rome, *Mostra d'Arte Missionaria* in 1950, stands comparison, for tragic intensity, only with Romanesque sculpture.

A powerful impression is often made on Europeans by the 'demonic' quality of African masks. A mask is, however, not only the expression of demonism, that is to say,

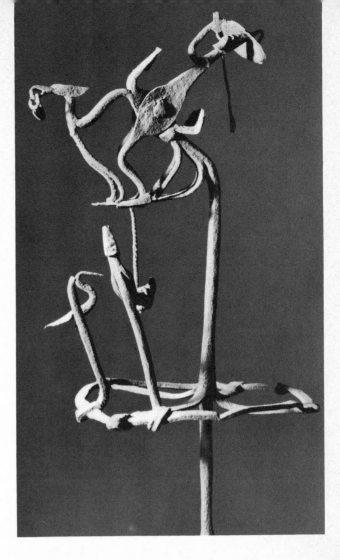

of the belief in demons that dwell in the human soul and are depicted in the mask. The mask is much more a means whereby these demons can be vanquished. It is not simply a representation of a demon, but a means of exorcism through the act of representing it. The tremendous psychological power of the African manner of coming to terms with the demons within us has never been understood in Europe. Equally misunderstood are the marks of a triumphant struggle against the demons in the composure and dignity of African royal statues and ancestor figures. Demons cannot be denied or rejected but must be battled with if one is to obtain personal serenity. The European mind has never understood this typically African form of spiritual development. The European, who himself is grotesquely incapable of sublimating his own demons, is pleased to think of the African as a 'savage'.

This misjudgment of Africa and Oceania by Europeans was also evident in the field of art. As late as the end of the nineteenth and the beginning of the twentieth century the great collections of ethnological material in Belgian, French, British and German museums were still regarded as curios rather than as art. Around 1905, however, the Fauve painters in France and the Expressionists in Germany both discovered African and Oceanic art, mainly in these ethnological collections. This was at a moment when European artists and thinkers were turning away from what they felt was the falsity and superficiality of the culture of their time, and the confrontation with primitive art

103. **Benin openwork copper bracelet.** Nigeria. h. 5⅛ in. (13 cm.).

104. **Benin brass panther.** Nigeria. h. 16½ in. (42 cm.).

105 (below). **Ashanti brass 'kuduo' (divination bowl)** from Ghana. h. 4¼ in. (11 cm.). All Museum für Völkerkunde, Munich. In its metalwork (which itself may owe something Mediterranean stimuli in prehistoric times), W. Africa appears as the meeting point of many influences: Benin panthers (104) are reminiscent of the hunter style in rock pictures; the antithetical arrangement of the figures on the bracelets (103) recalls motifs from Oceania and Peru (plate 45); while the figures on the *kuduo* have been linked with Etruscan bronze vessels.

acted as a stimulus for much-needed freshness, strength and vitality. For the next ten or fifteen years, this interest extended to all other primitive forms of expression. Thus, in his *Demoiselles d'Avignon* (1906–7), Picasso turned to the archaic Greco-Spanish forms of Iberian sculpture, while the *Blaue Reiter* group in their 1911–12 exhibition in Munich, and especially in their epoch-making 1912 Almanac, reproduced primitive and folk-art forms from different regions and levels of world culture.

With the wider dissemination of a knowledge of primitive styles, other artists became involved. But where the artists of the pre-war period had tended to be emotive in their outlook and their aspirations, the artists of the nineteen-twenties, embittered by disillusion, turned to the expression of inward psychological rather than outward emotional values. In the work of Paul Klee and Joan Miró we can see the search for and inner vision leading to striking resemblances with the rock art of the early hunters which are anything but accidental. Klee and Miró were familiar with all aspects of primitive art, and this is by now true of the majority of contemporary artists in all parts of the world. There is little doubt that primitive man, so long regarded by the west as a backward element and a merely economic factor, has now emerged as a vital influence. If it was his artistic message which was first felt by Europeans, the economic and social achievements of primitive man still remain to be fully appreciated.

Further Reading List

General

Adam, Leonard *Primitive Art.* Cassell, 1963

Bacon, Edward (ed.) *Vanished Civilizations.* Thames & Hudson and McGraw-Hill, 1963

British Museum *Handbook to the Ethnographical Collections.* 2nd ed. Oxford, 1925

Fraser, Douglas *Primitive Art.* Thames & Hudson and Doubleday, 1962

Giedion, S. *The Eternal Present: the Beginnings of Art.* Oxford University Press, 1962

Piggott, Stuart (ed.) *Dawn of Civilization.* Thames & Hudson and McGraw-Hill, 1961

Stone age

Bandi, H. G.; Breuil, H.; Berger-Kirchner, L.; Lhote, H.; Holm, E.; Lommel, A. *Stone Age.* Methuen and Crown, 1961

Frobenius, Leo and Fox, Douglas C. *Prehistoric Rock Pictures in Europe and Africa.* From Material in the Archives of the Research Institute for the Morphology of Civilization. Frankfurt-on-Main, New York, 1937

Graziosi, Paolo *Palaeolithic Art.* Faber & Faber, 1960

Kühn, Herbert *The Rock Pictures of Europe.* Sidgwick & Jackson and McGraw-Hill, 1956

Lommel, A. *The World of the Early Hunters.* Cory, Adams and Mackay, and McGraw-Hill, 1966

Maringer, Johannes and Bandi, Hans-Georg *Art in the Ice Age.* George Allen & Unwin, 1953

Shamanism

Manker, Ernst M. *People of eight seasons: The Story of the Lapps.* (Studio) Viking, 1963

Vorren O. and Manker, E. *Lapp Life and Customs.* Oxford, 1962

Çatal Hüyük, Anatolia

Mellaart, James *Earliest Civilizations of the Near East.* Thames & Hudson, 1965

Mounted Nomads and Central Asia

Boroffka, G. *Scythian Art.* London, 1928

Kšica, Miroslav *Rock Pictures in Central Asia.* Science and Life No. 3. London, 1960

Mongait, Alexander *Archaeology in the U.S.S.R.* Penguin Books, 1959

Phillips, E. D. *The Royal Hordes.* Thames & Hudson and McGraw-Hill, 1965

Rostovtzeff, Mikhail *The Animal Style in South Russia and China.* Princeton, 1929

Bronze age in Europe

Hawkins, Gerald *Stonehenge Decoded.* Souvenir Press and Doubleday, 1966

Early China

Andersson, J. G. *Symbolism in Prehistoric Painted Ceramics of China.* Kegan Paul, 1929

—, *Topographical and Archaeological Studies in the Far East.* Kegan Paul, 1939

Chêng Tê-k'un *Archaeology in China*, I, II, III. Heffer, 1964

Li Chi *Examples of Pattern Dissolution from the Archaeological Specimens of Anyang.* Artibus Asiae, Vol. XXII, 1/2.

—, *The Beginnings of the Chinese Civilization.* University of Washington, 1957

Loehr, Max *Chinese Bronze Age Weapons.* Cresset Press and University of Michigan, 1956

Sirén, Oswald *Histoire des Arts de la Chine.* Paris, 1929

New Guinea and Melanesia

Cranstone, B. A. L. *Melanesia: A Short Ethnography.* British Museum, 1961

Museum of Primitive Art *The Art of Lake Sentani.* ed. S. Kooijman. New York Graphic Society, 1959

Oceania

Anell, Bengt *Contributions to the History of Fishing in the South Seas.* Studia Ethnographica Upsaliensia. Uppsala, 1955

Buck, Sir Peter H. (Te Rangi Hiroa) *The Coming of the Maori.* Whitcombe & Tombs

Bühler, Alfred and others *Oceania and Australia.* Methuen, 1962

Linton, Ralph and Wingert, Paul *The Art of the South Seas.* New York, 1946

Shapiro, H. L. and Suggs, R. C. *New Dates for Polynesian Prehistory.* Man, Vol. LIX, Art. 3, London, 1959

Australia

Davidson, David S. *Aboriginal Australian and Tasmanian Rock Carvings and Paintings.* Memoirs of the American Philosophical Society. Vol. V. Philadelphia, 1936

Hammond, J. E. *Winjan's People.* Perth, 1933

McCarthy, Frederick D. *Australian Aboriginal Decorative Art*, 4th ed. Australian Museum Handbook. Sydney, 1956

Mountford, C. P. *Aboriginal Paintings from Australia.* London, 1964

Schulz, Agnes *North-West Australian Rock Paintings.* Memoirs of the National Museum of Victoria. Melbourne, 1956

Unesco World Art Series *Australia—Aboriginal Paintings—Arnhem Land.* New York, 1954

America

Covarrubias, Miguel *The Eagle, the Jaguar and the Serpent.* Knopf, 1954

Douglas, Frederick H. and d'Harnoncourt, René *Indian Art of the United States*. New York, 1941

Fewkes, Walter J. *A Prehistoric Island Culture Area of America*. 34. Report. Bureau of American Ethnology. Washington, 1922

Heizer, Robert F. and Baumhoff, Martin A. *Prehistoric Rock Art of Nevada and Eastern California*. University of California, 1962

Kothrop, S. K.; Foshag, W. F.; Mahler, Joy *Robert Woods Bliss Collection: Pre-Columbian Art*. London, 1957

Schuster, Carl *Human Figures with Spiral Limbs in Tropical America*. Miscellanea Paul Rivet Octogenario Dicata II. Mexico, 1958

—, *A Survival of the Eurasiatic Animal Style in Modern Alaskan Eskimo Art*. Chicago, 1952

Walter, H. V. *Archaeology of the Lagoa Santa Region (Minas Gerais)* Rio de Janeiro, 1958

Steward, Julien H. *Petroglyphs of the U.S.A.* Annual Report of the Smithsonian Institute, Washington, D.C., 1937

Africa

Bleek, D.; Rosenthal, Eric; Goodwin, A. J. H. *Cave Artists of South Africa*. Cape Town, 1953

Clark, J. Desmond *Third Panamerican Congress on Prehistory*. Livingstone 1955. London, 1957

Clark, J. D., Cooke, C. K. and (ed.) Summers, R. *Prehistoric Rock Art of Rhodesia and Nyasaland*. Chatto & Windus, 1960

Fagg, William *Tribes and Forms in African Art*. Methuen, 1966

Lajoux, J.-D. *Rock Paintings of Tassili*. Thames & Hudson, 1963

Lhote, Henri *The Search for the Tassili Frescoes*. Hutchinson, 1958

Motifs

Neumann, Erich *The Great Mother*. Routledge and Kegan Paul, 1960 Pantheon Books, 1955

Rhyd, Hanna *The Symbolism of Mortuary Ceramics*. Bulletin of the Museum of Far Eastern Antiquities, Vol. I. Stockholm, 1929

Salmony, Alfred *Antler and Tongue, An Essay on Ancient Chinese Symbolism and its Implications*. Artibus Asiae, Supplementum XIII. Ascona, 1954

Sankalia, H. D. *The Nude Goddess or "Shameless Woman" in Western Asia, India and South-Eastern Asia*. Artibus Asiae, XXIII. Ascona, 1960

Schuster, Carl *Joint-Marks*. Koninklijk Instituut voor de Tropen, Mededeling No. XCVI, Afdeling Culturele en Physische Anthropologie, No. 39. Amsterdam, 1951

Shun, Shen-ling *Human Figures with Protruding Tongues found in the Taitung Areas*. Bulletin of the Institute of Ethnology, Academia Sinica, No. 2. Taipeh, 1956

Other books and periodicals from which line drawings have been copied:

Andersson, J. G. *Research of the Prehistory of the Chinese*. B.M.F.E.A. No. 15. pl. 189, 1. Stockholm, 1943 (Figures 59*a-b*, 60*a*)

Bossert *Geschichte des Kunstgewerbes, Skythische Kunst*. p. 153, No. 2. Berlin, 1928 (Figure 40)

Jefferson, Christiane *Dendroglyphs of the Chatham Islands*. Fig. 119. Wellington, N.Z. (Figure 60*c*)

Karlgren, B. *Bronzes in the Wessén Collection*. B.M.F.E.A. No. 30, pl. 37e. Stockholm, 1958 (Figure 59*c*)

Manker, Ernst *Die Lappische Zaubertrommel*. Vol. 2, p. 28. (Figure 7*e*)

Mountford, C. P. *Aboriginal Decorative Art from Arnhem Land*. Adelaide, 1939 (Figures 31*d, e*)

Mountford, C. P. *Aboriginal Bark Paintings from Field Island, Northern Territory*. Adelaide, 1957 (Figure 31*c*)

Röder, Josef *Felsbilder und Vorgeschichte des McCluer-Golfes*. Darmstadt, 1959 (Figure 31*b*)

Schuster, Carl *Genealogical Patterns in the Old and New World*. Revista do Museu Paulista, N.S. Vol. X, p. 7–123. São Paulo, 1956–58 (Figure 52)

Snoy, P. *Asiatische Felsbilder*. I, No. 2. Umschau, 1961 (Figure 7*f*)

Steinen, K. von den *Die Marquesaner und ihre Kunst*. Vol. I, fig. 121. Berlin, 1925 (Figure 60*b*)

Index

The numbers in heavy type refer to colour plates; italic numbers refer to black and white illustrations.

Acknowledgements

The publishers gratefully acknowledge the consent of the following to reproduce subjects illustrated in this book:
The Frobenius Institute, Frankfurt-am-Main. *Colour:* 84, 87, 89, 92; J.-D. Lajoux, from his book *Tassili-n-Ajjer*, Les Nouvelles Editions du Chêne, Paris. *Colour:* 82; H. V. Walter, Belo Horizonte, Brazil. *Black and white:* 8; Museum für Völkerkunde, Munich, for all objects from their collections reproduced in this book.

Photographs were provided by the following:

Colour: British Museum, London 60, 76, 96; Cleveland Museum of Art 22; Dornauf Graphik, Frankfurt-am-Main 84, 87, 89, 92; Dumbarton Oaks, Washington, D.C. 11, 34, 75, 78; Hans Hinz, Basle 1, 4, 5, 6, 8, 13; Michael Holford, London 7, 9, 12, 20, 21, 23, 24, 25, 26, 27, 29, 30, 31, 32, 33, 35, 36, 37, 38, 39, 40, 41, 42, 43, 44, 45, 46, 47, 48, 49, 50, 51, 52, 54, 55, 56, 57, 58, 59, 62, 63, 64, 66, 67, 68, 69, 70, 71, 73, 74, 77, 79, 80, 81, 91, 93, 94, 95, 97, 98, 99, 100, 101, 102, 103; J.-D. Lajoux – Rapho, Paris 82; Henri Lhote, Paris 83, 86; The Robert H. Lowie Museum of Anthropology, University of California 10; MAS, Barcelona 3; James Mellaart, London 18, 19; Museum of the American Indian, Heye Foundation 65, 72; Museum für Völkerkunde, Munich 28; Peabody Museum, Harvard University 53; Queen Victoria Museum, Salisbury,

Rhodesia 85, 88; Rietberg Museum, Zürich 17, 90; Tom Scott, Edinburgh 61; Achille B. Weider, Zürich 2, 14; Wettstein & Kauf, Zürich 17, 90;

Black and white: Aerofilms, London 25; Archives Photographiques, Paris 22; Australian News and Information Bureau 37; Bayerisches Landesamt für Denkmalpflege, Munich 19; Bord Failte Eireann, Dublin 26; British Museum, London 28, 29, 45, 46, 73, 74, 76, 77, 101; Forman, Prague 21; Paolo Graziosi, Florence 13, 15, 90; Michael Holford, London 14, 36, 44, 47, 48, 49, 51, 53, 54, 55, 56, 57, 61, 63, 64, 66, 67, 68, 69, 70, 71, 72, 75, 79, 80, 82, 83, 86, 87, 88, 89, 92, 93, 94, 95, 96, 97, 98, 99, 100, 102, 103, 104, 105; D. Hughes-Gilbey, London 65; Hunterian Museum, Glasgow 78; Landesmuseum Joanneum, Graz 27; Malta Government Tourist Board, Valletta 24; MAS, Barcelona 1, 16, 17; B. Moosbrugger, Zürich 91; Museum of the American Indian, Heye Foundation 81, 84, 85; Museum für Völkerkunde, Basle 58, 62; Museum für Völkerkunde, Munich 12; National Museum, Athens 18, 23; Sakamoto, Tokyo 35; Naturhistorisches Museum, Vienna 20; Rietberg Museum, Zürich 70, 91; Tromsø Museum 4; Universitets Oldsaksamling, Oslo 7, 11; Videnskapsselskapets Oldsaksamling, Trondheim 10; Derek Walter, Belo Horizonte, Brazil 8; Achille B. Weider, Zürich 2, 3; Yan, Paris illustration on p. 7;

See also page 172

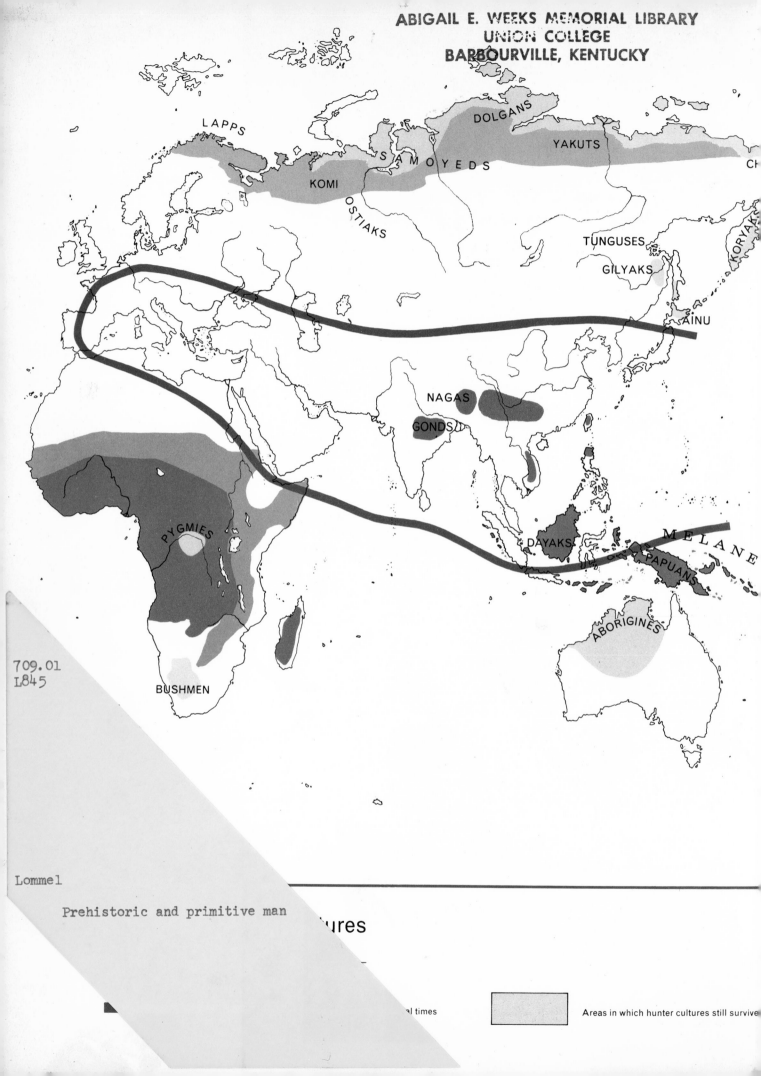

LAPPS

DOLGANS

YAKUTS

KOMI

S A M O Y E D S

OSTIAKS

CH

TUNGUSES

GILYAKS

KORYAKS

AINU

NAGAS

GONDS

PYGMIES

DAYAKS

M E L A N E

PAPUANS

ABORIGINES

BUSHMEN

ures

al times

Areas in which hunter cultures still survive